Publish
&Flourish

Become a Prolific Scholar

Publish & Flourish

Become a Prolific Scholar

Tara Gray

An earlier version of some of these ideas appeared in

Gray, T. (1999). Publish, Don't Perish: 12 Steps to Help Scholars
    Flourish. *Journal of Staff, Program, and Organization
    Development (16)*4, 135–142.

1st printing • June 2005

2nd printing • September 2006

3rd printing • June 2010

Printed in the United States by BookMasters, Inc.,
Ashland, Ohio.

THE TWELVE STEPS

Acknowledgments

Jean Conway formatted the book and made possible its publication through the New Mexico State University Teaching Academy. I have come to think of Jean as my partner in all things.

Many people have read and responded thoughtfully, including the following experts: Robert Boice, SUNY–Stony Brook; Wendy Belcher, Princeton University; Gregory Colomb, University of Virginia; Peter Elbow, University of Massachusetts; Kenneth Henson, The Citadel; Deirdre McCloskey, University of Illinois at Chicago; and Joseph Williams, University of Chicago.

Six writing groups of New Mexico State University (NMSU) faculty also read and commented on various stages of the book.

Three NMSU faculty read the book both in its infant stage and again in later iterations: Suzanne Buker, Communication Studies; Ereney Hadjigeorgalis, Agricultural Economics; and Deborah LaPorte, English.

Laura Madson, Department of Psychology at NMSU, was willing to "drop everything" to read sections again and again over an eight-year period. Few writers have such a friend and colleague.

Jane Birch, from the Faculty Center at Brigham Young University, has been my partner in this project every step of the way. Every year since 1999, she has directed her own highly successful version of this program .

I could not have written this book alone. I could have written something, of course, but it would have had more problems and less promise. I thank you all.

About the Author

www.taragray.com

Tara Gray serves as associate professor of criminal justice and as the first director of the Teaching Academy at New Mexico State University. The Teaching Academy provides NMSU educators with training, mentoring, and networking.

Dr. Gray was educated at the United States Naval Academy, Southwestern College in Kansas, and Oklahoma State University. She earned her Ph.D. in economics by asking, "Do prisons pay?" She has published many scholarly manuscripts, including three books. She has been honored at NMSU and nationally with seven awards for teaching and service.

Dr. Gray regularly presents the workshop *Publish & Flourish: Become a Prolific Scholar.* She has presented it to 6,000 scholars in more than 25 of the United States and in Mexico, Guatemala, and Saudi Arabia. Workshop participants report that she is "spirited, entertaining, and informative–she's anything but gray!™"

Why I Wrote This Book and Why You Should Read It

As a writer, I've had some hard knocks myself. I wrote my dissertation and published my first paper without incident. As I worked on my second journal article, I kept careful records of the time spent. I discovered I worked more than one hundred hours *per page.* This was on the writing only, after the data were collected and the numbers were crunched. I sent the paper to ten of the best-known experts in the world and five responded. They seemed to like it. I made the changes they suggested and I thought the paper was finally ready to go. I sent it out for review, and this is what came back, in red ink, half an inch high:

> *This paper is:*
>
> *"very poorly done."*
>
> *"a very badly prepared piece of work."*
>
> *"plagued by myriad problems."*
>
> *"so badly written that few persons will have the patience to try to make sense of it."*

I knew just what to do. I cried. But when I was done crying, I marched myself up to my office to revise the paper. I ignored the insults and forced myself to respond to each specific comment. Responding to the comments took four and one-half hours, which was less than one-half of one percent of the time spent on the entire paper. Then I fired the paper off to an equally good journal, where it was accepted without revision (Gray, 1999, p. 140).

I knew there must be a moral to the story; I decided there were three. One moral was clear: Even if the reviewer dislikes your work, ignore the overall assessment, but respond to each specific comment. Remember the old adage, "Don't throw the baby out with the bath water." I learned something else: Don't write too long alone. I should have had others read and respond to my work far earlier in the writing process, perhaps after two hours or ten hours per page. There was a third moral. My paper was poorly organized and the editor's comments read like a paint-by-number kit: "Move this here; move that there." The editor saw bad organization that the experts hadn't seen. It was transparent to the experts. They weren't reading to understand–they already understood. The third moral became clear: Ask less expert readers to read drafts of your work (from a workshop with Joe Williams). They will see problems of organization and clarity more easily and they will read your work more like the editor of the journal you are likely to send it to. In contrast, the experts that I sent it to looked right past poor organization because they weren't reading to understand–they already understood.

As you can see, I learned about writing at the same school that you probably did: the School of Hard Knocks. But it's not the only school, or even the best. Much is known about how to become more prolific–and any scholar can. Even when you can't work harder, there are important ways to work smarter. Therefore, I decided there should be a program to help scholars flourish. Naturally, it's a twelve-step program because writing is difficult and writing well is a lifetime project. Writing can feel like one step forward and two steps back–like walking up the down escalator. The steps break writing down into little tasks that any writer can do.

Much research shows that the steps work if you work the steps. Robert Boice, a social psychologist, did the basic research on the two most important steps. He is the guru of scholarly writing and the author of four books and many articles on the subject (see for example Boice, 1989, 1990, 1994, 1997, 2000). He spent much of his career proving the importance of ideas that would become the two central steps of the program: writing daily as well as keeping records of your minutes spent writing and holding yourself accountable to someone for doing so. He showed that these steps are important regardless of discipline, teaching load, or type of institution (Boice, 1989, 1997). In one of his studies, a group of scholars wrote the way they had always written–occasionally, in big blocks of time. The group wrote or revised a mean of 17 pages per year. Another group wrote daily, kept records of their time spent writing, and held themselves accountable to others for writing daily. This group wrote or revised a mean of 157 pages per year or nine times as many pages (Boice, 1989, p. 609).

The steps work if you work the steps. I am occasionally confronted by someone who says that the steps don't work. When this happens, I always ask the same question, "For how long did you try the steps, especially the most important one about writing daily?" The answer is never measured in months or weeks or even days. The answer is always, "I wasn't able to write daily." My response is always the same, too, "Then how do you know the steps don't work?"

Deciding to work the steps is difficult for academics because we are trained skeptics. We are trained to question everything– from the size of the sample to the quality of the data. Naturally, you question whether the twelve steps are the one best way to write. Although one size doesn't fit all, the steps give you a writing system to try on for size. When you try on each step, you broaden your range of skills as a writer. In this way, even steps you don't adopt permanently make you a better writer for having tried them. Think of it as an empirical question: The only way to know whether the steps work is to try them.

Every scholar can become more prolific, and these steps can show you how:

Managing Time
1. Differentiate the "urgent" from the important.
2. Write daily for 15–30 minutes.
3. Record time spent writing daily–share records weekly.

Writing
4. Write from the first day of your research project.
5. Post your thesis on the wall and write to it.

Revising
6. Organize around key sentences.
7. Use key sentences as an after-the-fact outline.

Getting Help
8. Share early drafts with non-experts and later drafts with experts.
9. Learn how to listen.
10. Respond to each specific comment.

Polishing and Publishing
11. Read your prose out loud.
12. Kick it out the door and make 'em say "No."

My challenge to you is this: Work the steps and see how they work in your life. And every time you fall off the writing wagon, keep coming back (and back and back!) to the steps that can make writers great.

Managing Time

— 1 —
Differentiate the "urgent" from the important

— 2 —
Write daily for 15–30 minutes

— 3 —
Record time spent writing daily– share records weekly

Managing Time

Many faculty members get caught up in the busyness of working every day, which leaves us feeling "intense, impatient and overscheduled" (Boice, 1997, p. 22). When asked, "Is this the busiest year of your life?" 55 percent of faculty answered "yes" (Boice, 1989, p. 606). When one group of faculty members were asked to estimate how much time they work per week, they estimated that they worked a mean of almost 60 hours per week, including almost 30 hours on research. Next, these same faculty members were asked to keep records of their workweeks by jotting down every 15 minutes whether or not they were working. After they kept records, they reported working a mean of 29 hours per week, including 1.5 hours spent on research and one-half hour spent writing (Boice, 1989, p. 606). So these faculty members were working 30 hours per week and worrying another 30.

Once the faculty kept records, they reexamined their earlier, exaggerated estimates of time worked. They thought these estimates came from their previous assumption that the busyness they felt could only have come from long workweeks (Boice, 1989, p. 607). Upon reflection, they were "forthright with admissions that they were not nearly as busy as they had supposed" (Boice, 1997, p. 21). They discovered that they rarely had days without some relatively free period, which they usually used for a low-priority activity such as checking their mail, reading the newspaper, or talking on the phone. These relatively free periods could be used for more important tasks–such as writing–so that working could be more productive and relaxing could be more restful.

These faculty also needed to stop seeing busyness primarily as a status symbol. Busyness is a status symbol, to be sure. Some academics actually compete to be the "busiest" (Gray, 1999, p. 137). "You think your day was busy? Wait 'til I tell you about *mine!*" Busyness is a status symbol, but it is also a way of being *victimized* (Gray, 1999, p. 137). Faculty who stagger around under their heavy loads of research, teaching, and service–complaining constantly–are not empowered but are out of control of their time and their lives (Boice, 1997, p. 22). One writer put it this way: "What was most important for me [was] to stop complaining and finding excuses" (Boice, 1994, p. 77). To stop complaining about your many duties, ask yourself who put them there and decide to make better decisions. Take control. "Become a manager of your time, not a victim of it" (Gray, 1999, p. 137). Remind yourself that time is the great equalizer–we all have different levels of power, money, status, and intelligence, but we all have 24 hours in every day–you, me, and the President of the United States.

Step 1
Differentiate the "urgent" from the important

It has been said that life is composed of the urgent, the important, and the trivial. We exhaust ourselves on the urgent, seek rest in the trivial, and forget the important (Webb, 1996–1999). What is the difference between the urgent and the important? Important activities move you closer to your goals, have serious consequences if left undone, and require you to act on them. Urgent activities seem to need to be done right now, but they act on you and you react to them (a ringing phone, a beeping e-mail, a knock at the door).

Studies show that faculty who may lose their jobs if they do not prioritize well still spend more time teaching and less time researching than they believe their institution expects and than they personally prefer (Menges, 1999). Why is that? Teaching and (some) service are clearly both urgent and important; as a result, they tend to take priority over research:

> Teaching pressures are immediate, and the rewards are concrete. Research pressures are extremely non-immediate, and the rewards are subtle—there's no thunderous applause—and very slow in coming…. I co-wrote a paper in 1979 that today has 400 citations. In the first five years, I received zero comments or acknowledgment whatsoever. (Harrison, as cited in Goldman, 2001)

In academe, "research may not be urgent, but it is certainly important" (Gray, 1999, p. 138). Our job as time managers is to ensure that we do not neglect important activities. The next two chapters present strategies for creating a sense of urgency around your writing because urgent things get done.

___ Step 2 ___
Write daily for 15–30 minutes

Writing daily, even for 15–30 minutes, greatly increases scholarship productivity. Those who write infrequently in big blocks of time often write in "binges" (binges are writing periods that last more than three hours). In one study, the group of participants who wrote daily for 15–30 minutes wrote twice as many total hours as those who wrote in binges but generated ten times as many published articles (Boice, 2000, p. 144). The group that wrote daily was five times more efficient.

But, you say, "What's wrong with binging?" "I get writing done. I'm successful and respected" (Boice, 1994, p. xx). True, many people write in binges and some are successful. But binging is difficult to sustain because it causes burnout, which decreases the motivation to write again the next day or week (Boice, 1994, p. 4). You should write daily if you want to be more prolific, to write more with less anguish, or to take the "journey to comfort and fluency" (Boice, 1994, p. ix). One writer explained it this way: "The most important thing I realized is that I have to write daily, daily, daily! All else takes care of itself if I avoid binging and just write daily" (Charles Knutson, personal communication, August 11, 2004).

Do not wait for the inspiration to write. William Faulkner said, "I only write when I'm inspired. Fortunately, I'm inspired at 9 o'clock every morning." Inspiration follows the practice of regular, accumulated work (Boice, 1994, p. 19). Write daily and the inspiration will follow:

> Days off are deadly. One follows another, and all too soon fears creep back in. Nothing is as easily delayed as writing. The thoughts available today, the ideas ready to flow, will not be bestowed tomorrow. Tomorrow's shipment may be equally good. It may even be better. But today's ideas, as they would have been expressed today, are probably gone. (Shaughnessy, 1993, p. 6)

Once you commit to writing daily, you may still wonder how can you write anything meaningful in just 15 minutes. Do not underestimate the power of a single minute. One physician-poet, William Carlos Williams, turned out a large body of work during office hours by writing single lines of poetry between patients (Carroll, 1969, p. 90). The more often you write, the less time it takes to "start up." With practice, you will find you can start quickly and accomplish much in just a few minutes a day–but only if you wrote yesterday. Scholars who insist on big blocks of time didn't write yesterday. Nonetheless, many scholars still hold stock in BIG BLOCKS OF TIME, INC.™ To write daily, you must sell your stock. If you resist, ask yourself this question: When was the last time a big block of time dropped in on you? When you wait for large blocks of time, first you'll wait for summer, then sabbatical, then retirement (Boice, 1997, p. 21). Don't wait; set aside a short block of time to write today.

To write daily, you must give something up, select a time and place to write, decide how to get started and how to stop the interruptions. What will you give up to write? Examples of good things to give up: 15–30 minutes a day of newspaper reading, TV watching, web surfing, emailing, and so on. Examples of bad things to give up include sleep and exercise. Boice (1994, p. 103) found that most people will not give up sleep to write. It turns out they would rather sleep than write. The only people who had any luck with altering their sleep habits to write were those who got up earlier—and went to bed earlier.

Next, choose a time to write. Ideally, this should be at the same time every day, preferably first thing in your day or work day when you "are most awake and clear" (Boice, 2000, p. 139).

> The most important skill I learned was the habit of writing for a half hour first thing when I get to work. I completed two papers (both accepted) and the rough draft of a paper that has been hanging over my head for years. And much of this was accomplished in a half hour per day. (Gray & Birch, 2001, p. 275)

Another writer says, "I feel good now about getting my writing done before I go to campus. It puts me in a bright mood for the day" (Boice, 2000, p. 140).[1] The advantages of doing the most important things first are legendary, "First things first." Or, as my mother liked to say, "What you do first every day gets done."

But what if you are a night person, not a morning person? Boice (1994, p. 104) found that virtually all writers were successful when writing in the morning. Alternately, you might try writing at night and see what happens. If you write on Monday night, no need to write on Tuesday morning. If, however, you fail to write

---

1   You may wonder how to clear time for writing in the mornings. Here's how one writer managed:

> It all began when I noticed that I normally lay abed after awakening for about 15 minutes. Before, it had seemed essential, nonnegotiable, until I simply got by with less and less. [Now] I'm content with a few minutes. Then I noticed that I spent 20 to 30 minutes sipping coffee and reading a newspaper. And that I often took time to run errands on my way to work in the morning. Those, too, I could see, took away time for writing in the morning.... Now I read the papers in the evenings when I'm tired and little good for more. (Boice, 2000, p. 140)

on Tuesday night, force yourself to write on Wednesday morning and Wednesday night to get back on your night writing schedule.

Once you have chosen a time to write, make a writing date with yourself. Write it in your planner. When someone asks you if you can attend a meeting at that time, look in your planner and say, "No. I have an appointment." Take your appointment seriously. Just as you occasionally break dates with others, you may have to occasionally break this date with yourself, but the key word here is "occasionally." Take your commitment to yourself and your research agenda as seriously as you take your commitments to others.

Next, choose a writing place. Write in the same place every day, and preferably in a place where nothing but writing is done and a place that is quiet with few distractions:

> The most fluent, healthy writers… set aside a room or location where *nothing but writing* is done (i.e., with few distractions such as magazines or televisions nearby, often not even phones or electronic mail)… The essential thing, they told me, was to keep the writing context as simple and serene as possible. (Boice, 2000, p. 139)

Now, decide how to start your writing session each day. It is hard to sit yourself down to write daily when you are not in the habit. It's difficult to face a blank paper every day when you are used to putting it off until you're close to a writing deadline. "It's always tempting… to turn to something less threatening, less demanding, less frantic, less tiring" (Boice, 1994, p. 4). Every writer needs a "BIC lighter," where "BIC" stands for "Butt in Chair," the lighter that starts the fire (Deborah LaPorte, personal communication, March 24, 2010). And, remind yourself of the empirically proven importance of writing daily.

Once you have started, you must learn how to stop the interruptions, including internal interruptions. Internal interruptions are difficult to stop because writing is hard and distractions are easier. "Once planted at the desk… you will find your subconscious drawing on various reserves to persuade you to stop: fear, boredom, and the impulse to track down that trivial point by adjourning to the library…. Don't." (McCloskey, 1985, p. 196; 2000, p. 20). Now that "the library" has moved into your office in the form of the Internet, the problem of stopping your writing to look up "just one thing" is even more problematic. But the solution is still the same: Don't.

To help you fend off internal interruptions, you may want to use two sticky pads and one reward. On the first sticky pad, record all your potential distractions (Deborah LaPorte, personal communication, March 24, 2010). Consider it a "data dump." For example, "Thaw chicken for dinner" or "Rescue son from day care." On the second sticky pad, alert yourself that your writing minutes are beginning by jotting down the exact minute you are starting to write. Making this notation will remind you that you are about to focus intensely on writing for a few minutes. Once you stop writing, you should again make a note of the time. Having finished your writing for the day, you can then reward yourself by allowing yourself to respond to your e-mail. Don't read your e-mail first. E-mail is like a black hole: The more you send, the more you get back; the more you get back, the more you send.

You must also stop external interruptions. To avoid external interruptions, the American novelist John Cheever put on a business suit and wore it to the basement, where he hung it on a hanger and wrote in his underwear (Keyes, 1995, p. 141).

I bet he didn't have many interruptions. To avoid external interruptions, you must turn off the ringer on your phone—not to mention the "beeping" on your computer that tells you that "you've got mail." If you work on campus, close your office door and post a sign on it (Boice, 1997, p. 24). Consider, "Police Line Do Not Cross. Scholar confined to quarters as a subject in a study on research productivity. Feel free to knock after _____ [time]" (Scott Ferrin, personal communication, March 25, 2010). (E-mail me at tara@taragray.com for a copy of the stop sign, which you can print in color for maximum effect.) Once you have posted the sign, place a sticky note on it that shows the time the office will open. In sum, do whatever it takes to write daily: Unplug your telephone, change the locks on your doors, tell the baby to go away or grow up (McCloskey, 1985, p. 199, 2000, p. 31). *Do whatever it takes.*

Record time spent writing daily–
share records weekly

Daily writing won't become a reality for you unless you keep records of your daily writing and hold yourself accountable to someone for writing daily. What difference does keeping records make? In one study, all the participants attended workshops with Robert Boice, who explained the importance of writing daily and keeping records of minutes written. At the end of the workshop, one group of program participants continued to write the way they had always written, which was occasionally, in big blocks of time. Another group agreed to write daily and to keep daily records of their time spent writing. Without records, it's too easy not to write on any given day–and to convince yourself that you will write "tomorrow," but "tomorrow" never comes, or at least it doesn't come very often. By writing daily and keeping records the second group was able to outperform the first group by a factor of *four.*

In the same study, a third group of participants took the same measures as the second group (writing daily and keeping records), but this group also held themselves accountable to someone for writing daily. What difference does it make to also hold oneself accountable to others? The third group wrote more than the first group by a factor of *nine* (Boice, 1989, p. 609). The numbers look like this in pages written or revised per year: 17 pages by the group that wrote in big blocks of time, 64 pages by the group that wrote daily and kept records, and 157 pages by the group that also held themselves accountable to others (Boice, 1989).

Table 1

**Daily Writing, Record Keeping, and Accountability:
The Effect on Productivity**

(Boice, 1989, p. 609)

Participant Groups	Mean Pages Written or Revised per Year
First Group (chose to continue to write occasionally, in big blocks of time)	17
Second Group (agreed to write daily for at least 15 minutes and record it)	64
Third Group (agreed to write daily for at least 15 minutes and be held accountable for doing so)	157

Yet another study of this phenomenon took place with one group of participants over two years. In the first year, participants wrote occasionally in big blocks of time. In the second year, the participants wrote 15–30 minutes daily, kept records, and held themselves accountable to others. The percentage of participants who finished manuscripts rose from 10% in the first year to 100% in the second year (Boice, 1997, p. 25). So writing daily and keeping records will increase your productivity by a factor of four–and if you also share those records with others, it will increase your productivity by a factor of nine or ten.

After reading statistics like these, you may wonder why every scholar doesn't keep records. But you may also resist keeping a writing log because it seems too rudimentary, because you are not sure what to count as writing, and because you are not sure how to keep a log. Fortunately, each of these challenges is easy to overcome. Keeping a log is rudimentary, but it's also effective and you have to weigh the one against the other. One scholar wrote, "The writing log reminded me to write. And reminded me I had written." Another wrote, "The writing logs were the absolute key to my success… it was like standing on the scales, I didn't always like what I saw but I knew I could always do something about it!" (Joanne Bentley, personal communication, June 16, 2004). If you are still not convinced, remind yourself that, "Many great writers, Hemingway among them, kept charts of their progress" (Boice, 2000, pp. 142–143). I tell myself that, if keeping records was good enough for Hemingway, it is good enough for me!

What counts as writing versus research time? "Research" is generating something to write about. You may spend time reading, designing surveys, collecting data, crunching numbers, or designing and running lab experiments. Your research can be done daily in 15-30 minute increments, right before or after your writing, or it may be done occasionally in big blocks of time. The key here is to keep your research minutes separate from your writing minutes and to minimize your research minutes and maximize your writing minutes for greater productivity. In contrast to research, "writing" is explaining research in words you can save. You may jot down ideas, outline, or write, revise, or edit paragraphs that you hope will someday be a part of a paper. You may also work on the final presentation of numbers (not their generation) for a table or chart.

In the end, however, there are some gray areas, so only you can decide how you measure your writing time. Take reading, for example, which should count as research but is sometimes done while one is writing. If you can look up a statistic or a quotation quickly and type it into your text, you may count that time as writing. If, however, you pick up an academic article and get lost in it, spending your full 15 minutes of writing time reading the article, then you should count that time as research. What about thinking? Does time spent thinking count as writing time? In my view, no. Instead of allowing yourself to "think" for any significant part of your 15 minutes, I would encourage you to alternate thinking with getting your ideas on paper so that most of your writing time is spent writing. One test I use to see whether I'm writing is the video camera test. If a video camera were filming me while I'm trying to write, would people watching the tape think I was writing?

Once you decide how to measure writing time, how and where do you record your minutes? I recommend that for the first three months you join a writing club and record your minutes online at *www.academicladder.com.* The beauty of a writing club is that you record your minutes written each day and a few words about your writing process and how well it went. Twice a week the leaders of the club write you back with an encouraging word. This is a wonderful way of forming the daily writing habit over three months or so. The writing club is directed by Dr. Gina Hiatt and Ms. Jayne London. It costs about $70/month and is well worth every penny.

After the three-month period, you may no longer want to record your minutes online. Instead, you may use the detailed writing log that appears at the back of this book (see *Appendix A*). This log has the advantage of asking you several questions about your application of the 12 steps beyond just recording your minutes. Whatever type of log you use, you may want to keep a printed version of it next to the place that you write because its mere presence will remind you to write.

Once you have kept records, who do you share them with, how do you go about it exactly, and how long does all this take? Share your records with someone daily for the first three months, then weekly after that. Share your records with a sponsor or buddy: someone who has agreed to help you work the steps, especially the step that requires writing daily. Just like other 12-step programs, the only way to work this program is to get a sponsor or buddy. I learned this the hard way. About 30 months before this book went to print, Stephen Covey spoke in my town. I was extremely busy at the time. I was changing careers for the second time in ten years. I was traveling all over the country to give workshops on the subject of this book, and I was holding down three jobs, including one full-time job. I was also applying for a new job. At the workshop, Stephen Covey said something that made an indelible impression on me. He said, "To know it and not to do it is not to know it." I could feel the word "FRAUD" written in large purple letters on my forehead. No matter how much I was working, I could not believe that I was traveling across the country extolling the benefits of writing daily—but not writing daily myself. I got a sponsor immediately. It is that sponsor, Dr. Jane Birch of Brigham Young University, who is responsible for my success as a writer today. I thank her.

You too will need a sponsor or a buddy and that person should have certain characteristics. On the one hand, he or she should understand the absolute importance of writing daily. (If there is any problem here, just show your sponsor or buddy the relevant sections of this book.) He or she should hold your feet to the fire, without resorting to shaming or blaming. Your sponsor or buddy may be a colleague, spouse, or friend. He or she may or may not be a writer. In either case, there is no expectation that your sponsor or buddy reads your work. He or she is only responsible for responding to your success or failure at writing daily.

What is the difference between a sponsor and a buddy? A buddy shares his or her minutes of writing with you. As a result, you are doing each other a favor and you are not beholden to your buddy the way you are to a sponsor. If your buddy stops writing, you will need a new buddy or sponsor. On the other hand, your relationship with a sponsor is not reciprocal. That is, your sponsor does not report his or her daily writing minutes to you. Then, your sponsor can be there for you regardless of his or her own writing success or failure.

You may now see the value in having a sponsor or buddy but think it will take too much time. Your relationship with your sponsor or buddy does not have to take much time and the payoff will be huge. I write my sponsor each Sunday. I write a quick note—"I wrote seven days for 105 minutes total. Good week this week." I estimate that I can keep records of my time spent writing—and correspond with my writing sponsor—in about ten minutes per week. I am not alone in thinking that having a writing sponsor helps me write. One writer explains, "Just having to tell someone the silly excuses I have for not working on my research helped me quit allowing it to happen" (Gray & Birch, 2001, p. 275). Over time, I have found my sponsor to be the single biggest reason that I keep going on my writing projects when the chips are down or when I'm traveling. I have promised to write daily, and I simply don't want to let my sponsor down. So stop thinking of writing as a solitary activity and start searching for your writing sponsor or buddy. Once you find someone who works for you, keep that person for life.

Writing

— 4 —
Write from the first day of your research project

— 5 —
Post your thesis on the wall and write to it

Writing

Now that you have carved out the time to write, you want to get words on paper efficiently, but elitism often interferes. A former president of the American Psychological Association talked about those few of us who "deserve to write"–by which she meant those few who have something worth saying (Boice, 2000, p. 112). Many less established academics adopt this view, too. We frequently proclaim that "most of what gets published" falls far below our own high standards (Boice, 1997, p. 20). The problem with elitist views is that if you judge the finished work of others so harshly, it is difficult to be kind to yourself and your own first drafts. As a result, elitism can silence you and cause you to become a "silent writer" (Boice, 1997, p. 20). This is elitism at its worst: setting unrealistic standards that few can meet, including yourself.

Instead, think of yourself as a publishing scholar, control your negative self-talk, and learn to play both the "believing game" and the "doubting game." Thinking of yourself as a publishing scholar may be the single most important habit of a working academic (Gebhardt, as cited in Olson, 1997, p. 52). Tell yourself that you are more alike than different from the most prolific scholars.

> The people who say the most profound, intelligent, or witty things are the same as us… They've pushed themselves through fearful situations and told themselves they could make it… We're all working with approximately the same material–humanity. It's how we feel about ourselves that makes the difference. It's what we tell ourselves that makes the difference. (Beattie, 1987, p. 113)

Avoid negative self-talk. Although negative self-talk seems to come naturally to writers, one study found that a group of scholars could change their self-talk by using a simple technique. During their writing sessions, this group wrote down the negative things they said to themselves—their self-talk—and by doing so, they became more conscious about how they talked to themselves. This group of writers reduced their negative self-talk by 40 percent in three months (Boice, 1994, p. 75). What do you say to yourself as a writer? To find out, monitor your self-talk during your writing sessions. Write down the negative things you say to yourself—anything that is not encouraging. Begin to consciously adjust what you say. Don't apologize for your writing, not even to yourself (Boice, 2000, p. 131). Turn your internal critic off—or, if that is impossible for you, turn it down a little bit.

Learn to play both the believing game and the doubting game (Elbow, 2000, pp. 76–80). As writers, we must play the doubting game by reading our papers critically and asking the tough questions such as, What's the point? Will anybody care about this? But the doubting game is for revision. It's an important game, and every writer must play it—but not before the paper is drafted. To draft a paper, we must play the believing game. To play the believing game, we allow ourselves to write without self-censorship, while reassuring ourselves that we have a point to make even if it isn't yet readily apparent. "Be selfish for a while about the little candle of creation you are tending, however poor it may seem beside the conflagrations of the giants" (McCloskey, 1985, p. 199–200). Remind yourself that every scholar has something to say. "You have something to say. Just write it down" (Gray, 1999, p. 136).

Write from the first day of your research project

Everybody knows that you should finish the literature review—and the entire research project—before "writing it up." Everybody is wrong. Neither the literature review—nor the research—is ever finished. I tried to finish a literature review once. For my dissertation, I collected an entire file drawer full of articles, alphabetized by author and abstracted on index cards. When an internationally known scholar complimented my literature review, I should have known I had overdone it. Nonetheless, I was embarrassed to learn later that I had failed to include one of the most important articles on my topic. Naturally, it was written by my new department head—and published in the number one journal in my field! My literature review was not really finished, was it? I learned then what I know now: No literature review is ever finished. It was not finished then, it is not finished now, and it never will be (Gray, 1999, p. 136).

Instead of trying to finish your literature review, try to streamline it. Streamline it by writing first and then reading (Drake & Jones, 1997, p. 31). Write from within, from what you feel and know. You will write faster and with a more authentic voice—your own. Because you have thought about your discipline for years, how much is your thinking going to change by reading one more article (or doing one more day of research)?

As you write, leave "holes" in your prose to be filled later, "Find a statistic to support this point: _____" or "Find an opposing point of view" or "Find this citation:

_____." Once you have drafted something, turn to the literature and begin "reading-to-write" (Flower et al., 1990). Reading-to-write is far better than conducting a literature review of the "general and often wasteful sort that precedes most writing projects" (Boice, 2000, p. 128). When reading-to-write, your reading is sharply focused, which means you read quickly. Otherwise, most of what you read will turn out to be irrelevant to your paper (McCloskey, 2000, p. 29). Most scholars read "to learn." Don't. Read to write. Read to fill in the holes of an already drafted paper (Boice, 1997, p. 29). One writer (John Talbot, personal communication, June 15, 2004) explains it this way:

> I've learned to resist the temptation to read every book and article on a given topic before I deign to add my two cents. Much better to get the paper going first, to write my say, and then to survey the literature to see if anybody else's opinion supports, contradicts, mitigates, or, in the most dire cases, cancels my own.

This writer is smart to do his own thinking before reviewing the literature.

Don't wait to start writing until you finish the research, either. Streamline your research by writing–informally– throughout the project. All writing need not be formal and nearly finished, as for example, a certain paragraph within a certain section of a certain paper. Instead, think of writing as something you do to generate thought and to keep a record of your ideas, however crude, so they can be reviewed and revised later. The crudest writing about a given idea is superior to the best thinking precisely because it can be saved, reviewed, and revised later (Gray, 1999, p. 136). As you write, imagine you are writing a letter: "I don't know why I got the results I got in the lab today... Perhaps it was because... No, I don't think so. I think the reason was… Tomorrow I will try something different." One physicist (Dallin Durfee, personal communication, June 15, 2004) explained how writing this way improved his research and saved him time in the end:

> I've begun to write about my physics experiments while they are still in progress, allowing me to see weaknesses in our experiments and realize what data will be most useful in making cohesive arguments early on, before research time has been wasted on unfruitful ideas.

So write from the first day of your research project—as soon as you have a research idea. Don't finish the research first; research as you write, and write as you research.

____ Step 5 ____
Post your thesis on the wall and write to it

When you sit down to write, take a stab at describing what you are going to write about. Start with something simple, your topic, just a word or phrase even. You can develop this into a sentence later. Ultimately, this will be the sentence that often begins, "In this paper, we…" Ultimately, you could send this sentence as a telegram because it will capture your central idea (Williams, 1990, p. 98). Don't make this difficult by trying to write the perfect sentence. Just jot down something quickly for now.

Know that your first effort is only a working thesis. You can change it at any time—you can and you should. Better theses will arise from the writing process. Keep coming back to your thesis. Work back and forth between your thesis and the rest of your paper—revising first one and then the other. Eventually, you will want to develop a thesis sentence that is short and memorable and tells your reader what is at stake, what problem you are trying to solve, what claim you are making, or what your result or conclusion is. Post your thesis on the wall and write to it. Better yet, post it in the header or the footer of your paper where you will be invited to read it again and again. Having your thesis in front of you will help you define, refine, and write to your purpose.

Having posted your thesis prominently, consider exploring it further through free writing, free talking, outlining, or some combination. Consider using free writing, which many experts argue is the best and easiest way to get your words on paper (Elbow, 1998, p. 13). Free writing means writing whatever occurs to you in a stream-of-consciousness style without stopping and without self-censorship. "You can't really draft freely and keep going unless you welcome nonsense and garbage. No treasures without garbage" (Elbow, personal communication, February 10, 2005). Writers who are new to free writing start by writing for a very short time, such as three to five minutes, and work up to somewhat longer periods, such as 15 minutes. Free writing generates momentum (Boice, 1994, p. 96). Ideas seem to come without struggle and some of these are both surprising and useful (Boice, 1997, p. 28). After you free write, you can "see" that you discovered the main points on the page. E. M. Forster (1973, p. 101) put it this way, "How can I know what I think till I see what I say?" If free writing sounds strange to you, remember that it is like something you already know how to do: free talking. Sigmund Freud started working with his patients by asking them to free write, but he found free talking easier to elicit and sustain (Boice, 2000, p. 131). As a writer, you may decide to take advantage of this. Robert Boice spent many hours watching scholars write, and he observed that the most successful, fluent scholars did not write silently. They "thought aloud," and they read sections of their prose as they wrote it and after they wrote it. As a result, when you sit down for a 15- to 30-minute writing segment, you may want to try free talking about your subject for a few minutes. Saying your ideas out loud before you type them up will improve your fluency and the quality of your work. Saying your words out loud after you write will also help. "Don't write entirely silently, or you will write entirely stiffly" (McCloskey, 1985, p. 199; 2000, p. 30).

Compared to free writing or free talking, you may already prefer another approach to getting your ideas on paper:

outlining. Or, as you experiment more with outlining, you may come to see the advantages of outlining that others have noted (Boice, 1994, Chapter 2). You may discover that writing an outline is just as easy as making a list and reordering it in a logical way. You may also discover that writing from an outline saves the strain that comes from having to discover what you want to say while saying it (Boice, 1994, p. 53). One writer tried writing projects both with and without outlines and reported, "When you have done the… outlining well and imaginatively, the writing is a snap. It's really just rewriting because you don't have to struggle to find ideas, just to say them a bit more clearly" (Boice, 1997, p. 70). You may conclude that writing from an outline is a faster way to complete a project overall.

If you already have an established habit of outlining or freewriting or freetalking, by all means use it. If you don't have an established habit, experiment with outlining, free writing, and free talking. See which one works best for you in various stages of your writing projects. For me, outlining works best when I know the points I want to make; freewriting or freetalking works better when I have yet to discover the points I want to make. Whatever method or combination of methods you use, keep your thesis posted in plain view and work back and forth between your thesis and your prose, revising first one and then the other.

Revising

Revising

The problem with revision in academic writing is that there is not nearly enough of it: Editors and authors share the blame. Editors at academic journals are generally scholars who serve as volunteers. They are chosen based on their scholarly expertise, with no training as editors. Naturally, many of these volunteers don't feel compelled to help authors with their writing. "The editors themselves do not edit. At the least they might reveal to the young that rotten writing causes more articles to be rejected... than rotten *t*-statistics" (McCloskey, 1985, p. 188).

To make matters worse, scholarly authors sometimes display a "cynical disregard" for advice—even from editors and reviewers. Authors seem to disregard advice because they believe that complicated ideas cannot be stated simply. Some academics even write turgid prose as a way to demonstrate the complexity of the ideas. One scholar, Denis Dutton, gives an award to the worst published sentence, and each year, a truly terrible sentence wins. The following is one such sentence (and yes, it's all one sentence):

> Indeed dialectical critical realism may be seen under the aspect of Foucauldian strategic reversal—of the unholy trinity of Parmenidean/Platonic/Aristotelean provenance; of the Cartesian-Lockean-Humean-Kantian paradigm, of foundationalisms (in practice, fideistic foundationalisms) and irrationalisms (in practice, capricious exercises of the will-to-power or some other ideologically and/or psycho-somatically buried source) new and old alike; of the primordial failing of western philosophy, ontological monovalence, and its close ally, the epistemic fallacy with its ontic dual; of the analytic problematic laid down by Plato,

> which Hegel served only to replicate in his actualist monovalent analytic reinstatement in transfigurative reconciling dialectical connection, while in his hubristic claims for absolute idealism he inaugurated the Comtean, Kierkegaardian and Nietzschean eclipses of reason, replicating the fundaments of positivism through its transmutation route to the superidealism of a Baudrillard. (Bhaskar, as cited in Dutton, n.d.)

As Dutton put it, "To ask what this means is to miss the point... [Authors like this one] hope to persuade their readers not by argument but by obscurity... Actual communication has nothing to do with it" (Dutton, 1999, p. 11).

C. Wright Mills (1959, pp. 218–219) argued that such convoluted prose was a result of the academic "pose":

> Such lack of intelligibility, I believe, usually has little or nothing to do with the complexity of subject matter, and nothing at all with profundity of thought. It has to do almost entirely with certain confusions of the academic writer about his own status... [Because the academic writer in America] feels his own lack of public position, he often puts the claim for his own status before his claim for the attention of the reader to what he is saying... To overcome the academic prose you have first to overcome the academic pose.

To overcome the academic pose, scholars should stop trying to show how complex our ideas are in a vain attempt to show how important we are.

Instead, we should get serious about communication, which means we should get serious about revision. For years, my own revision "system" consisted of reading my prose again and again and working to make it "sound better." Using this "system," I managed to spend up to 100 hours writing a page. I was responding to the "critic on my shoulder" that said the page could always be improved. This is true, but it's better to get a finite number of comments from real readers and then send the paper off, as discussed in the next chapter, than to keep responding to a critic with infinite criticisms. Writing on one page for 100 hours was not a revision system—it was a non-system. Even if you don't have a good revision system, it will be easy for you to learn to use one because, as a scholar, you have already done a great deal of writing and learned much about writing well.

To develop a revision system you should bear in mind that papers should be well written at three main levels, and each level serves a different function (Rankin, 2001, p. 100). At the macro level, the paper should communicate its purpose clearly to its audience. The macro level is the most important level, which is why you post your thesis prominently so you can't help but write to it. At the mid level, paragraphs should be consistent in structure and length and, most important, the organization should be clear both within and between paragraphs. At the sentence level, sentences should be well worded and grammatically correct. As long as there is still work to be done at the paper or paragraph level, do not allow yourself to take time to improve prose at the sentence level. The sentence level is the least important level and should be revised last.

At the mid level, paragraphs should be consistent in structure and length. Such paragraphs suggest to the reader that the writer is in charge and leading the reader confidently through what is known (Baker, 1984, p. 52). The length of paragraphs in scholarly work should be about half a page long on a double-spaced page—or "square." The expected length varies somewhat by discipline. Paragraphs are longest in the humanities, shortest in the sciences, and somewhere in between in the social sciences.

In any discipline, paragraphs should not vary much in length and be "long enough to complete a thought, short enough to give the reader some visible hope of relief, and middling enough not to look odd alongside its fellows" (McCloskey, 1985, p. 205).

A paragraph should also be consistent in structure; that is, it should complete three functions in order. First, the paragraph should open with a transition. (Do not close paragraphs with transitions as you may have been taught to do in school. Transitions are now thought to belong in the beginning of paragraphs.) The transition can be as short as a word or a phrase that was used in the previous paragraph–or as long as a sentence or even two or three (Williams, 1990, p. 101). Second, the transition should be followed by a topic or key sentence. Third, the rest of the paragraph should provide support or evidence for the idea in the key sentence. As you revise, you should check each paragraph against this template and not break it unless you have a reason for doing so.

—— Step 6 ——
Organize around key sentences

Readers expect nonfiction to have one point per paragraph. Ideally, the point of the paragraph should be suggested in one sentence, a key or topic sentence, located early in the paragraph and supported by the rest of the paragraph. A key sentence is to a paragraph like a street sign is to a city: It orients the readers and helps them navigate. A key sentence is much like a topic sentence: It announces the topic of the paragraph (Williams, 1990, pp. 97–105). A key sentence must be broad enough to "cover" everything in the paragraph but not so broad that it raises issues that are not addressed in the paragraph. After you think you have located the key sentence, ask yourself the (key) question: "Is the rest of the paragraph about the idea in the key sentence?" Ideally, the key sentence should announce the topic simply and with little detail; it should announce the topic without trying to prove the point–the rest of the paragraph serves that function. The key sentence should be short and memorable, although many of the key sentences we read fall short of ideal. The ideal key sentence should include key words in its subject; that is, if the topic of the paragraph is "Napoleon," then "Napoleon" should appear as the subject of the key sentence, rather than "he."

A key sentence differs from what many people were taught about topic sentences because a key sentence need not be the first sentence in a paragraph (Williams, 1990, pp. 90, 101). The later the key sentence appears in a paragraph, the longer the paragraph tends to be. When writers take longer to warm up to the key sentence, they also take longer to explain, support, and qualify it (Williams, 1990, pp. 92–93). How long writers take to warm up is mostly a matter of tradition and different disciplines have different traditions. In most scientific disciplines, key sentences tend to be the first sentence in each paragraph. Key sentences are often the second sentence in the social sciences and sometimes even the third sentence in the humanities. In all fields, key sentences can be the last sentence in the paragraph, but then they require anticipatory key sentences that are placed early in the paragraph and provide a foreshadowing of what the key sentence is to be. It is usually easier to state the key sentence early in the paragraph because we are not mystery writers.

Find the key sentence as you read the following paragraph: Once you have made your choice, read the explanation that follows.

Example. "We learn rules for actions better when those rules are structured, whether we learn by practicing them, by watching a teacher demonstrate them, or by listening to a teacher explain them. But do we learn better from a demonstration or an explanation? We are likely to learn more when we watch a demonstration if our language skills are so weak that we cannot understand words easily, or if the teacher cannot verbalize the rules. We are also likely to learn more from watching a demonstration when we must quickly coordinate intricate actions such as learning to ride a bicycle, but the explanation for them is too cumbersome. Finally, we are likely to learn more from a demonstration if the action is difficult or unfamiliar and the teacher lectures about it at length. On the other hand, we will learn an action better from an explanation if we can deftly translate explanations into actions and then store the information." (Williams, 1990, p. 87).

Explanation. The second sentence is key: "But do we learn better from a demonstration or from an explanation?" Everything after this key question addresses the issue: In which situations do we learn better, from a demonstration or an explanation? The first sentence is probably serving as a transition from the previous paragraph.

Now, pause here to get more experience with finding key sentences in other sample paragraphs before proceeding further. *Appendix B* provides a series of the examples from a variety of fields with increasing levels of difficulties. The advantage of these examples is that the answers appear right after the examples. In contrast, you will spend the rest of your life as a writer wrestling with examples from your own prose when the answers are less than clear. Therefore, it is advantageous to work through these examples, which provide the one time you will actually have answers to your questions. [Turn now to *Appendix B.*]

Next, practice finding key sentences in your own paragraphs. Don't expect your reader to take time to "piece together" a key sentence from phrases in different sentences. Piece it together for your reader. If you can't find your key sentence immediately, your reader won't be able to find it at all (Booth, Colomb & Williams, 2003, p. 213). If this is the case, write a simple sentence that expresses your topic and place it early in the paragraph. Then, revise your paragraph around it.

Just as every paragraph needs a key sentence to be coherent, every paper and every section of a paper must have one. Your paper already has a key sentence: It's the thesis you posted on the wall or in your header or footer. Next, make sure every section of your paper has a key sentence: the introduction, the literature review, the methods section, and so on (Booth et al., 2003, p. 210). Sometimes smaller sections of a paper—two or more closely related paragraphs—will also require a key sentence.

Because sections have their own key sentences, paragraphs can sometimes have two key sentences, with each sentence serving a different function: One sentence might serve as key for the section while another serves as key for a paragraph. For example, the first two sentences of a paragraph might say, "Next we will compare the nutritional value of the apple and the orange. First, consider the orange." In this paragraph, the first sentence is probably working as a key sentence for the next two paragraphs, but the second sentence is working as a key sentence for the paragraph on oranges. A paragraph can legitimately contain two key sentences only when key sentences serve different functions. Any other time, one idea should be dropped or two paragraphs should be written.

___ Step 7 ___
Use key sentences as an after-the-fact outline

You have identified a key sentence in each paragraph as a way of checking the internal organization of the paragraph. To examine the organization between paragraphs, list your key sentences—and headings—so they provide an after-the-fact outline (Booth et al., 2003, pp. 188, 213; Foss & Waters, 2007, pp. 274-275). Of course, you could list your key sentences first and then compose your paragraphs around them. Even if you compose your key sentences first, you will want to pull your final key sentences out of your prose to see the after-the-fact outline.

To see the after-the-fact outline, either cut and paste each of your key sentences into a separate document or use the "hidden text" function on your word processor to hide everything but the key sentences and the headings (see *Appendix C* for details). I recommend either of these methods over underlining the key sentences on the printed page because when I do that, I start reading the whole paper rather than just the key sentences and the headings.

Next, read just the list of sentences and question yourself about purpose and audience:

• How could the key sentences better communicate the purpose (thesis) of the paper to the intended audience?

Each and every key sentence should help you communicate the purpose to the audience. If any key sentence fails to help you do that, delete it or rewrite it immediately. Many of my initial key sentences are tangential to my purpose and when I discover that, I footnote them because it makes me feel better than deleting them outright. Of course, when I send it to a publisher, we all know what happens to footnotes!

Finally, read your list of key sentences one more time and ask yourself about organization:

- How could the key sentences be better organized? More logical? More coherent?

If any key sentence seems to be in the wrong place in the list, move it to make it more logical or more coherent. Keep moving key sentences around until the organization is tight.

Once you have viewed your sentences as an after-the-fact outline, you will see how valuable it is to view your prose through this new lens. Viewing your prose this way will give you a much tighter, more focused paper.

Your after-the-fact outline will help you to draft your abstract better and more quickly than before. To begin, start by reading all the key sentences and deleting the ones that don't belong in the abstract. Repeat that process until you have five to seven sentences remaining. Then, try rewriting the sentences so they are written to be read as a group. When you write an abstract this way, you may find that you can write a better abstract in an hour than you could previously write in a day. What has happened is that, by organizing your paragraphs around key sentences, you have learned a system of revision that helps you see the forest and not just the trees. You can explain your purpose clearly to your audience because you are clearer about your purpose. When you write your abstract, you don't have to struggle to find your key points because they are already isolated from the rest of the text.

Although key sentences may seem like a lot of work, the work pays off handsomely for you—and your readers. Key sentences within each paragraph serve as an outline of the paper—an outline that is accessible to the reader. This means that the time you spend improving your key sentences benefits the reader directly (because they appear in the prose) as well as indirectly (because they improve the rest of the prose).

Key sentences can benefit the reader even more directly if the writer is required to share the outline version of the paper with the reader. This is most useful to readers who are faced with reading much (inexpert) prose quickly, as teachers often are. As a teacher, you may want to capitalize on this by requiring your students to put their after-the-fact outlines on the cover page of each paper they submit. With this requirement, you will see an improvement in their writing and in the speed and accuracy of your grading. The outline immediately shows you the purpose of each student's paper and reveals problems with logic and coherence. This helps you because reading just each student's outline allows you to tentatively stack the papers into "A," "B" and "C" piles quickly and well by reading only the cover pages and thereby checking the thesis and organization. Then you can read the whole pile of "A" papers to make sure that all the papers in that stack have the same quality of evidence and therefore deserve the same grade. For more information about this and other techniques to improve student writing and your grading, contact me at tara@taragray.com.

Similarly, when you work with graduate students writing master's theses or dissertations, you may want to require the students to give you an after-the-fact outline of their working manuscripts. When I work with these students for 15 minutes each week, I read only their outline until it is in good enough shape to communicate the purpose of the manuscript logically and coherently. It is only then that I turn my attention to the manuscript that the outline represents. I find that this approach saves me hours (days!) because it helps me focus on the larger questions. For example, what is the purpose of the manuscript and how does each paragraph contribute to it? Is the organization both logical and coherent? Students tell me that the approach seems artificial at first, but over time they see the benefit because they observe that their own writing is focused and flourishing, while their peers are floundering.

Getting Help

__ 8 __
Share early drafts with non-experts and later drafts with experts

__ 9 __
Learn how to listen

__ 10 __
Respond to each specific comment

Getting Help

Academic authors get feedback through a process known as the double-blind review process. "Double-blind" means "doubly anonymous" because the reviewer doesn't know who the author is and the author doesn't know who the reviewer is. The anonymity means that reviewers feel completely free to say whatever they think of the piece—and to take out whatever frustration they are feeling at the time. Many do. Sometimes they (we) get mean:

> I'm sorry but you just don't know how to use the English language (in response to an untitled submission of Rudyard Kipling, 1889). (Bernard, 1990, p. 58)

> I do not see anything in this to convince me you can write either narrative or fiction (in response to *The Last of the Plainsmen* by Zane Grey, 1908). (Bernard, 1990, p. 44)

> I recommend that [you bury this] under a stone for a thousand years (in response to *Lolita* by Vladimir Nabokov, 1955). (Bernard, 1990, p. 71)

Writers must "brave the perfectionism and hostility of critics unparalleled in other social endeavors" (Boice, 1997, p. 19). "Writing at all takes courage. Submitting work for publication takes something closer to bravado" (Keyes, 1995, p. 99).

Indeed, reviewers are relentlessly negative, make different criticisms of the same paper, and regularly disagree on whether or not something should be published. Research finds that reviewers make "only broad statements—if any—about the positive features of papers" (Fiske & Fogg, 1990, p. 592). In contrast, reviewers make an average of nine criticisms per paper (Fiske & Fogg, 1990, pp. 591–592). And they routinely disagree on whether or not to publish a paper (Fiske & Fogg, 1990, p. 591). As writers, our response is predictable–we stop listening and start talking about how stupid reviewers are. Instead, we need to learn how to listen.

___ Step 8 ___
Share early drafts with non-experts and later drafts with experts

Share drafts of your work with real readers rather than imaginary readers. Don't try to conjure up a picture of "a reader on your shoulder" and write for that imaginary reader. Why? Because as hard as you try, you cannot effectively imagine your reader. Why not? When you read your own stuff, you are not really reading, but reviewing what you were thinking at the time (Booth et al., 1995, p. 202; 2003, pp. 208, 263). Therefore, you consistently overestimate what your reader knows. In fact, overestimating what your reader knows is the biggest source of communication problems. As a result, your reader is in trouble more than half the time (McCloskey, 1985, p. 192).

There is another reason to avoid writing for the imaginary reader on your shoulder. For many people (i.e., perfectionists) that reader is an eternal critic with an infinite number of criticisms. Kick that critic off your shoulder and stomp on him (Weiss, 2002)! Writing for an eternal critic is the perfect way never to finish your manuscript. I was writing for that reader when I managed to spend 100 hours per page after the data were collected and the numbers were crunched. I was reading my paper again and again to make it "better." Instead, a superior approach is to write it, find a key sentence in each paragraph, line them up and make sure they are all contributing to your purpose and audience and that they are all organized. Then, start sending your paper to a finite number of real readers, each of whom will have a finite number of criticisms. Make those changes and then kick it out the door! This process will speed you up considerably while improving the quality of your document. So start a dialog with your readers. Stop imagining what your readers know and start answering their stated questions.

Share more drafts of your work, starting sooner, than you ever thought possible. You may protest that this will take too much time but consider it a different way of spending your time, not an additional way. You will find that it will streamline your writing process because "others can quickly identify omissions and logical breaks that would take you weeks to figure out" (Belcher, 2009, pp. 7-8).

Share different drafts of your work with readers with different levels of expertise: non-experts, experts, and Capital-E Experts. Non-experts include anyone who does not share a terminal degree in your discipline, such as your spouse, undergraduate or graduate students, or colleagues in other disciplines. Experts include any scholar with a terminal degree in your discipline, including colleagues in your department now and those with whom you went to graduate school. Capital-E Experts include the best-known scholars in the exact area in which you are writing.

As you search for readers in each of the categories, think in terms of your friends—and your enemies. You probably have friends who can read usefully for you but:

> an even better way is to have an enemy. An enemy is willing to devote a vast amount of time and brain power to ferreting out errors both large and small, and this without any compensation. (Von Bekesy, 1960, pp. 8–9)

Do not ignore your enemies when thinking of possible reviewers. The journal editor who wrote me the nastiest review of my life–the one I quoted in the opening story of this book– became a regular reader for me. I realized that he was "onto me" as a writer and could put words to my organizational problems.

I sent him every paper I wrote–until he retired. He rejected all of them. But he would show me what was wrong with my papers and how to fix it–within ten days!

I made the corrections quickly and sent each paper to another journal. The second journal always took the paper! Was he my enemy–or was he my friend?

Start sharing drafts early–long before you send your paper out for review. When you share early drafts, you will get more and better feedback–at the point in your research that it will save you the most time. How early should you share your work? The best answer is this: as early as you can convince yourself to share it with your most supportive reader, such as your favorite colleague. How early should that be? It depends. Suppose you wanted to spend a year on a manuscript–perhaps the fourth month would be a good time to start sharing. This would mean you would work alone during the first three months. Then you would start working with the non-experts during months 4–6, experts during months 7–9, and Capital-E Experts during months 10–12. The point here is that getting help from your readers is going to take a high proportion of your time as a writer, and you need to plan for this and start early.

Share early drafts with non-experts. By sharing with non-experts, you can choose people you have absolutely no need to impress—and equally important—people who have no need to impress you. These people won't withhold questions to impress you with their knowledge. They don't fear that their questions will betray what they don't know. As a result, there is nothing they won't ask. And, because they understand less, problems with clarity and organization are more transparent to them. Prod these non-experts to think about clarity and organization by asking questions, such as "What passages were hardest to read or understand?" "Where did you feel lost or even just unsure about where you were going?" Avoid questions that can be answered with a simple "yes" or "no" because they do not invite further dialog. Consider the question, "Is the paper clear?" Many readers answer that question by saying, "Yes, it's clear." This is an unfortunate answer because it won't make the paper clearer. Instead, you want to ask questions that help you start a dialog with your readers.

If you want to hire a very skilled non-expert, consider Ereney Hadjigeorgalis. Personally, I wouldn't send anything to press without having her read it first. She is an excellent developmental editor, which means she improves paragraphs, sections, and whole papers. If you want a copy editor who improves style, or sentences, a suggestion for that service appears in the introduction to the section "Polishing and Publishing." Unless you are a non-native speaker, I would be much more concerned about having a developmental editor—which the journals don't provide—than a copy editor, which are usually provided by the journals. (If I were a non-native speaker, I would want to have both a developmental editor and a copy editor read my work before it went out for publication.) A page describing Ereney's work appears on the second page from the back of this book.

Share middle drafts with little-e experts. These experts can help you in some of the ways that non-experts can help you–as well as some of the ways that Capital-E Experts can help you. Little-e experts can help you with clarity and organization as non-experts can, but only if you make it very safe for them to ask questions about those topics. Because you have written this paper, you will know far more about the topic than they do. So you must make it safe for them to ask you questions. Once they do ask you questions, don't shift the focus from the clarity of your writing to the depth or breadth of their understanding. Work hard to make it safe for these experts to say, "I don't get this," without feeling that you will respond–or even think– "Well, you wouldn't" (Keyes, 1995, pp. 100, 102). Instead, assume that many of your readers will have the same questions as these experts. These experts can also help you by giving you ideas for what you should read and where to send your article, and they can help you get better known in your field by referring your work to others and so on. That is to say, little-e experts can help you in many of the same ways that Capital-E Experts can help you. For that reason, you should approach them in much the same way you approach Capital-E Experts as discussed next except that you can share earlier drafts with experts because you know them better.

Share near-finished drafts with at least two Capital-E Experts. Why do you want to send near-finished drafts to Experts when you could wait for them to read the final copy in print? Because they are far more likely to read–and engage with and cite–something that lands on their desk with a letter addressed specifically to them than with something that they find "in the literature." Why at least two Experts? Because they won't necessarily respond to you, no matter how you approach them. Therefore, approach the Experts by tailoring an e-mail specifically to each one by explaining how their work has informed yours and by asking specific questions aimed at the intersection of your work and theirs. Then, ask each Expert, "What articles should I read and cite that I haven't?" and "To which journal would you send this manuscript?" Volunteer to read and respond to a paper for them now or in the future if that would ever be helpful. Finally, explain that you are asking only for a "quick read" (Gray, 1999, p. 139) and would be delighted if they would spend even 20 minutes with your work. Then, ask them when you can expect to hear back from them. Getting a date from them lets you know when to send them the paper—and it lets you incorporate changes from other Experts before sending it to the next Expert.

To review, your letter to Capital-E experts should include the following elements and your letters to little-e experts should include as many of these as appropriate:

- Tailor a letter to each Expert individually
- Explain how their work has informed yours
- Ask specific questions aimed at the intersection of your work and theirs
- Ask "What articles should I read and cite that I haven't?"
- Ask "What journal would you send this manuscript to?"
- Mention that if they respond to you, you will acknowledge them in your paper
- Volunteer to read and respond to a paper for them now or in the future if that would ever be helpful

- Explain that you are asking only for a "quick read" of even 20 minutes

- Ask for a turn around within two or three weeks

See *Appendix D* for a sample letter to a Capital-E Expert.

I mentioned that, when you write to Experts, you should volunteer to read their work in return and you should ask them to read for you quickly. Both are important. I learned the importance of volunteering to read for the Capital-E Experts from Joe Williams at the University of Chicago. Before writing him I had learned much about writing from his books and had attended one of his workshops in Chicago. When I wrote my first paper on writing, I sent it to Professor Williams for feedback. I was less than 30 years old and writing one of the first papers of my life. I wrote to him with fear and trembling: D-e-a-r D-r. W-i-l-l-i-a-m-s: I am nobody and nothing at no-wheresville and I'm writing to you the great Joe Williams at the University of Chicago. Would you please read my first paper on writing [although my Ph.D. isn't even in rhetoric]? He responded by sending me his comments and by saying he would read and respond to my paper if I would read and respond to three of his latest chapters, as enclosed. When I read his letter, I realized that just as Professor Williams is an important part of my audience, I am an important part of his (albeit a different part)!

It is also important to get readers of all stripes to read for you quickly. If you are on tenure track, publishing before your tenure deadline is vitally important. This means that you are entitled, especially before tenure, to nudge your readers forward a bit when it comes to reading your papers. Therefore, whenever you approach readers, ask them when you can expect to hear back from them. Understand that you are actually more likely to get a response this way than with an open-ended request that invites your paper to get buried under other projects. Remind yourself that a quick read is about all you can hope for. If you wait for a long detailed read and copious comments, first you wait for summer, then for sabbatical, and then for retirement. Don't wait: get a (quick) read today.

___ Step 9 ___
Learn how to listen

Learn how to listen. To listen well, listen without judgment, keep your reader talking, and remember that when it comes to clarity, the reader is always right (Gray, 1999, p. 140). First, listen without judgment. Tell yourself that your reader's criticisms are not aimed at criticizing you but at helping you produce a publishable manuscript (Smaby, Downing, & Crews, 1999, p. 235).

> Listen to what your reader says as though it were all true. The way an owl eats a mouse. He takes it all in. He doesn't try to sort out the good parts from the bad. He trusts his organism to make use of what's good and get rid of what isn't. (Elbow, 1973, pp. 102–103)

Second, keep your readers talking (or writing, as the case may be). When your readers say something like "Nice job" or "Good work," don't let them stop there. Ask the readers to be specific about what they liked most and why and what questions they have and why. When they respond, avoid saying anything negative whatsoever, including words like "no" and "but." Instead, restate what they say and ask whether you got it right. Ask how you might make a change that would improve the paper. Consider your readers an invaluable source of information that you can best cultivate by saying, over and over, in different ways, "Say more about that."

Third, remind yourself that when it comes to clarity, the reader is always right (Gray, 1999, p. 140). "Clarity is a social matter, not something to be decided unilaterally by the writer.

The reader like the consumer is sovereign. If the reader thinks something you write is unclear, then it is, by definition. There's no arguing" (McCloskey, 1985, p. 191; 2000, p. 12). Resist the temptation to explain what you meant. Instead, propose other ways to say the same thing to see if the reader thinks these changes would be an improvement. As a writer you must write not just clearly enough that the reader can understand, but so clearly that she cannot possibly misunderstand (Quintilian, Book VIII, ii, 24, as cited in McCloskey, 2000, p. 12).

____ Step 10____
Respond to each specific criticism

There are two reasons that you may wish to dismiss readers' specific criticisms of your work. First, when reviewers dislike your work and recommend against publication, you may feel that their specific suggestions cannot be trusted, either. In contrast, the value of the comments is unrelated to whether or not the reviewers recommended publication of your work. Remember that reviewers' recommendations as to whether to publish or not are influenced by many factors, including their ideology and research interests. But their specific comments are useful regardless of their ideology or their research interests. Therefore, take each suggestion seriously and act on it if you can. Don't throw the baby out with the bath water.

Second, it is tempting to conclude that, because each reviewer makes different suggestions, there is no agreement on what would actually constitute an improvement (Fiske & Fogg, 1990, p. 597). This is not true, however. When researchers examined scholarly reviews, they found that reviewers gave good [specific] advice and did not contradict each other:

> Reviewers did not overtly disagree on particular points. Instead, they wrote about different topics; each making points that were appropriate and accurate.... In instances in which we consulted the original manuscript, we found no reviewer criticism with which we disagreed... it was very uncommon for an editor to indicate disagreement with a point made by a reviewer. (Fiske & Fogg, 1990, pp. 591–597)

Don't expect reviewers—or other readers—to make the same comments. Know that one reader will criticize the literature review, while another will find fault with the methods, and yet another will take umbrage with the findings (Gray, 1999, pp. 140-141). Know that if you make changes in response to each of these readers, you will improve the paper and reduce the chance that other readers will find fault with the manuscript. Think of each specific concern as a hole in your rhetorical "dam": the more holes you plug, the better your argument will "hold water."

We have discussed ways to get help from readers individually because doing so conserves the reader's time. Working with readers in a group is also powerful, however, and will change forever the way you work with readers individually. Writing groups usually meet face to face so they demonstrate the value of discussing comments rather than just reading the reviewer's cryptic comments and hoping you understand them. Indeed, in a group, you learn that when you work with readers by email in the future, you should ask probing questions: "Say more about that," or "Might you give me an example?" In a group, even when the person who made the original comment can't readily put words to feelings, someone else can often explain more. This explanation usually gives you the understanding you need to proceed with changes—rather than to ignore the comment altogether. To learn more about writing groups, see *Appendices E, F,* and *G.*

Polishing
and
Publishing

— 11 —
Read your prose out loud

— 12 —
Kick it out the door and make 'em say "No"

Polishing and Publishing

Before you let go of your prose, you will want to polish it to a fine shine. Polishing your prose requires revising at the sentence level, which you should do last. Revise at the sentence level last to avoid revising sentences that will later get cut. When you revise at the sentence level, you should think first in terms of the big picture for the sentence. To help you, I recommend the splendid book, *Style: Toward Clarity and Grace* (Williams, 1990).

Finally, it is time to turn away from the big picture of the sentence and focus on the grammar and punctuation details. At this time you may want to hire a copy editor for a more polished look. If you don't know who to hire as a copy editor, consider hiring Jerry Byrd, EdD. He does excellent work, with a short turnaround time and reasonable fees. He can be reached at *jerrybyrd@aol.com.* Before any editor lays eyes on your work, however, polish your prose by reading it out loud as you work up the courage to kick it out the door and make 'em say "No"!

____ Step 11 ____
Read your prose out loud

To polish your prose, you should read it out loud. Academic prose doesn't have to read like a novel, but it shouldn't read like an encyclopedia, either. Although your prose may never sound truly conversational, a step in that direction would be an improvement. If you write more the way you speak, "writing would have more vigor" (McCloskey, 2000, p. 30). Also, you can listen for excessive precision. Excessive precision interferes with clarity. "Clarity differs from precision... Much obscurity comes from an excessive precision that hides the main point among a dozen minor ones... One cannot say exactly what one means, for this life has not time" (McCloskey, 1985, p. 192). As you read your prose out loud, "run your pen through every other word. You have no idea what vigor it will bring" (Smith, paraphrased in McCloskey, 1985, p. 213; 2000, p. 70).

Ideally, you should read your prose out loud to someone–or have someone read it out loud to you. This will allow you to watch the expression of the other person to see when he or she is most interested, bored, or whatever. This can give you valuable information for further developing certain parts of your prose and for shortening and sharpening others.

Don't assume that there is no one in your life who would listen to you read or read for you. Consider family members and consider other writers who might be willing to make an exchange. Remember that whether or not the person is in your intended audience is far less important than whether you find somebody. If you can't bring yourself to ask for help with your whole paper, ask for help with your abstract, introduction, and conclusion. And read your prose out loud even if you read it to yourself.

Reading your prose out loud is important for all writers, including scientific and technical writers.

> I'd argue that even technical papers should be read aloud–that even sentences full of technical information can and should be "sayable." (Notice, for example, how lists or clauses full of complex mouth-clogging language won't ruin the sayability of a sentence if you put them at the end. This same principle means reworking sentences so that parentheses are also at the end.) (Elbow, personal communication, February 13, 2005).

Technical writing presents enough challenges to readers without skipping any of the necessary steps to make it easier. One of those steps is reading it out loud before kicking it out the door.

____ Step 12 ____
Kick it out the door and make 'em say "No"

You are almost ready to send your paper out but three obstacles remain: pride, perfectionism, and fear of rejection. Instead of fearing rejection, you should expect rejection and plan for it (Boice, 1990, pp. 108–109). Select three journals for every manuscript. As a young scholar, I was advised that, before mailing a paper off for review, I should address three envelopes. And stamp them. It's good advice. By choosing three journals, you have a long-term plan for your paper. If your paper is rejected at the first journal, you are prepared to send it to the second journal without the usual delay (Garcia, cited in Henson, 1999, p. 119). Just be sure to respond carefully to every specific criticism from the first set of reviewers before sending the paper off to the next journal.

Even with three envelopes addressed, fearing rejection is natural because faculty speak often about journals with very high rejection rates–and then recommend that, when choosing journals, you "start at the top" (Belcher, 2009, p. 102). Both of these myths deserve careful examination. Rejection rates are not exceedingly high at most journals. Only five percent of journals reject more than 90 percent of the manuscripts they receive giving you one chance in ten of publication. More typically, journals reject 40-60 percent of the papers submitted, giving you a one in two chance of publication (Association of Learned and Professional Society Publishers, 2000). Instead of focusing all our conversations on the (few) journals with the highest rejection rates, maybe faculty should talk to each other—and to graduate students—about more typical rejection rates.

As mentioned earlier, when selecting journals, new scholars are also advised to start at the top (Belcher, 2009, p. 102):

> Send your article to "the leading journal." If it gets rejected, send it to the second leading journal; if it gets rejected again, send it to the third; and so on. You may be eighty before you get published, but at least you started at the top. (Belcher, 2009, p. 119)

Instead of starting with the leading journals, start with appropriate journals. Don't be drawn "like a moth to a flame" to only the most prestigious journals with the highest rejection rates. Instead of automatically sending your papers to the leading journals, consider more modestly ranked journals (Thyer, 1994, pp. 27-28). Graduate students, in particular, would do well to acquaint themselves with more modestly ranked journals because students mainly read the work of the leading thinkers in the field (Belcher, 2009, p. 48). As a result, students often have "an exaggerated idea of what publishable quality is" (Belcher, 2009, p. 48).

I am asked frequently, "How do you find out how the journals are ranked?" Check *eigenfactor.org* and google™ "Thomson Reuters impact factor [discipline]" for two possible sets of rankings. You also might ask around because your colleagues may keep a set of rankings that they have seen. Finally, you might contact the "educational" journal in your field. From time to time, journals such as the *Journal of Economic Education* and the *Journal of Criminal Justice Education* publish journal rankings for their disciplines.

As you look for appropriate journals, you should consider themed issues. Consider themed issues because they often have far higher acceptance rates than other issues in the same journal, but they still carry the same "brand name." One journal editor reported that his themed issues had a higher acceptance rate by a factor of 4.5 (Henson, 1997, p. 783).

To select appropriate journals, look over your bibliography, ask experts, and query editors. Look over your bibliography to see where articles similar to yours were published. Your bibliography may include some of your best outlets, especially when articles were placed in specialty journals where reviewers would be comfortable with your topic and able to give you good advice. One of the biggest reasons writers give for going to the leading journals is to get good advice. In my experience, this may be the wrong reason. If you have certain readers that you want advice from, consider asking them directly. That's the most obvious way to get their advice. If what you want is informed readers of your paper because you think they will have a more favorable view of the paper, you are most likely to get those readers in a specialty journal.

Next, give your paper to a few experts and then to a few Capital-E Experts and ask, "Where would you send this if you had written it?" Finally, contact the editors of the three journals where you most want to submit your paper (Belcher, 2009, pp. 128-135; Gray, 1999, p. 141; Henson, 1999, pp. 108–112; Hollingsworth, 2002, p. 159; Moxley, 1997, p. 9; Olson, 1997, pp. 57–58). Write an email to these three editors before submitting your manuscript formally, which is sometimes called a "query." Note that you can send multiple queries but you can ethically submit your paper to only one journal at a time. As a result, one scholar calls sending multiple queries the "only legitimate way around the single submission rule" (Belcher, 2009, p. 131).

Many editors appreciate queries. One journal editor refers to writing these letters of query as his first law, "Query, always query" (Van Til, 1986, p. 19). Another editor likes query letters because it means he can send only those papers through formal review that should be sent through formal review—rather than following the rules of his journal and sending all papers through formal review. He explained:

> There are many "do's" and "don'ts" for authors but I'm convinced that the most common... error authors make is not to examine the publication to whom they submit their work. Yet, I frequently receive manuscripts, which are [clearly inappropriate for my journal and] I'm faced with the conundrum of either sending the manuscripts out to review, thereby taking up reviewers' time and straining their patience knowing full well that the manuscript will be rejected; or arbitrarily rejecting the manuscript myself, thereby breaking the house rules of the journal. The result is frayed tempers, a lot of work, elapsed time, and inevitable rejection for the author who may well have had his manuscript accepted, if it had been submitted to an appropriate journal in the first place. (Harker, 1982, pp. 121–122)

Nonetheless, you may hesitate to query editors, fearing that your paper will be rejected outright. Indeed, the editors may reject your paper, but you should query anyway because you are spared months of waiting for the same bad outcome. If a journal editor rejects your paper at the query stage it helps you because you were likely to receive "mixed" reviews. When reviews are mixed, who makes the decision? The editor! So, again, this editor has saved you months of waiting.

How do you query journal editors? Email the editors to say that you are interested in submitting your paper to the journal and want to know how well they think it fits the direction they are trying to take the journal. This is the crucial question because chances are good that the journal's mission was written before this journal editor was in place. What you are trying to get here is whether or not your paper fits the current direction of the journal. In your email, also include the title and the abstract of your paper and attach the full paper. Wait two weeks and resend the full request. If there is no response in yet another week, submit your paper to a different journal, which is likely to have a better turnaround time. Once your query is answered, however, be sure to thank the editor, whether or not submission is recommended: Even when a paper is "rejected" at this stage, the editor has done you a great favor by saving you months of waiting.[2]

You have planned for rejection, so don't let pride get in the way. Prepare yourself for something less than an outright acceptance when you query editors or when you submit an article. It is far more likely to have your paper accepted after a revise-and-resubmit or on submission to another journal than on your first try. In education, for example, about 15 percent of papers are accepted initially–but 75 percent are accepted after

---

2   Writers can also query editors much earlier in the process (Boice, 1994, p. 200). One author reported sending a two-page summary to the editor of a prestigious journal only to learn that the premise didn't fit the results [because the author had missed a crucial reference] (Boice, 1994, p. 203). Six weeks later this author submitted another conceptual outline and the editor liked it and the author is writing this paper. The author concluded, "The important thing is that I didn't spend a lot of time writing the wrong manuscript" (Boice, 1994, p. 203).

being revised and resubmitted (Henson, 1999, p. 134). In both cases, the acceptance occurs only after the author makes the suggested changes. What's a revise-and-resubmit, you may ask? When a paper receives a revise-and-resubmit, or "R&R" as it is sometimes called, it means that the author is required to make changes and resubmit the paper—without knowing whether or not the paper will be accepted after the changes are made.

Despite the high acceptance rate of revised and resubmitted papers, authors regularly fail to resubmit them (Henson, 1997, p. 784). Of course, sometimes it's even difficult to recognize an invitation to revise and resubmit from a rejection letter. One faculty member recalls taking a manuscript review course in graduate school in which editorial decision letters were shared so that students could learn to "distinguish outright rejections from revise-and-resubmit opportunities masquerading as rejections" (Brad Sagarin, personal communication, March 25, 2010). It is not always easy to tell which is which. Analyze your letters carefully to detect any possibility of resubmission. If doubt remains, show it to others or ask the editor directly. Promise yourself that you will always revise and resubmit when the journal editor gives even a hint of encouragement to do so among pages of insults. Don't let pride get in the way. Remind yourself that for publishing scholars, the failure to revise-and-resubmit is the cardinal sin (Kristie Seawright, personal communication, March 25, 2010).

Finally, keep your perfectionism in check. Avoid an uncritical allegiance to excellence or a fear of badness:

> Fear of badness is probably what holds people back from developing power in writing. If you care too much about

avoiding bad writing, you will be too cautious, too afraid to relinquish control. Whereas if you go all out for excellence and don't worry about the bad writing that comes with it, before long you will be able to produce writing that people will really want to read–even to buy. (Elbow, 1998, pp. 302–303)

You may say that your paper is not really done: It could be better. That's true today, it will be true tomorrow, and it will be true 100 years from now (Gray, 1999, p. 141). It's tough to know when "enough is enough." Artists are encouraged not to over-paint a picture and bury a good idea in a muddy mess (Becker, 1986, p. 131). And so it is for writers: You must find the balance between "making it better and getting it done" (Becker, 1986, p. 122). You've written it. A variety of experts and non-experts have read it. You've responded to their criticisms (Gray, 1999, p. 141)–it's time to kick it out the door (Becker, 1986, p. 121). Don't worry–if your writing needs more work, you'll get another chance. Anonymous reviewers are not known for being over-kind (Gray, 1999, p. 141). Your job is to write it and mail it. The reviewer's job is to tell you if it will embarrass you publicly (Gray, 1999, p. 141). You've done your job so make 'em do theirs: Kick it out the door and make 'em say "YES!"

Working the Steps

Stephen Covey says that everyone should spend time every day to "sharpen the saw"–not just doing more and more of what we do, but taking time to reflect on what we do and get better at doing it (Covey, 1989, pp. 287–308). Abe Lincoln was even harsher. He said, "If I had six hours to cut down a tree, I'd spend the first four sharpening my ax." As a writer, you are now wielding a sharper saw and a better ax. You are better prepared for the task of writing, which is good because writing is difficult and writing well is a lifelong project. Steps counter the difficulty: they break an overwhelming task into smaller, more manageable steps. Ideally, you should try each step on for size, but you can make incredible progress by starting to work on only a few. Write daily. Organize around key sentences. Get help from others.

Go through the motions of taking the steps until you succeed–"Fake it till you make it." Like anyone in a 12-step program, prepare to work the steps–not once or twice, but over and over again for a lifetime. You will find your voice. You will lose it, too, because writing is a constant challenge between triumph and struggle, followed by more triumph and more struggle. The most important step you take will be the one you take each time you fall off the writing wagon: Climb right back on and keep coming back–and back and back–to the steps that can make writers great!

Afterword: How I work the steps

I've been asked to describe how I actually work the steps. So here's how I work them, step by step. Almost daily, I remind myself that my writing will never be urgent but it is truly important. When I start to feel that writing is not important enough to make it on my agenda for a given day, I try to take the long view. I ask myself whether a 15-minute delay will really make the rest of the day untenable. For me, the answer is usually "no." On those days, I limit my writing to 15 minutes because that's all I can spare.

I try to write every day of the year, Saturdays, Sundays and holidays included, but I would say I average writing six days a week year-round. This is because I sometimes have bad weeks when I travel, and these drag down my average. Sometimes I feel discouraged because I'm not as successful at writing daily as some of the writers who wrote books emphasizing writing daily. For example, Frank Silverman and Bob Boice rarely missed a day of writing for any reason whatsoever over their entire careers . In contrast, I have written daily only since 2003. Nonetheless, as the years go by, I'm becoming more committed to writing daily.

I write at home in the mornings to minimize interruptions and to face the day with confidence. By writing at home, I can go to campus feeling that one third of my workday is behind me. And I face almost no external interruptions. Once in awhile my partner will want to show me something or ask me a series of questions and at some point I will say, "This is my writing time." But at home, almost all interruptions are internal, and my best way of keeping them at bay is to know that I have duly noted my beginning writing time on my sticky pad. It's like a ritual for me. Once I have noted that time on the pad, I know that this is my time for writing, not for emailing or for anything else.

I keep records of my writing minutes on the sticky pad that I keep next to my keyboard. On the left side of the pad I write the time I start writing, the time I stopped writing, and the total minutes written. On the right side of the pad, I also keep records of the minutes I spend exercising. Before I started keeping minutes of my exercising, I would have said I exercised daily. Upon further inspection, I realized that I said that because I *think* I *should* exercise daily. I decided to start keeping records of my exercise to see whether the reality matched the ideal. It turned out that I was exercising only twice a week! By keeping records, however, I have been able to increase my exercise to six days a week. So keeping records has the same effect on my exercise that it has on my writing.

I share these records with my sponsor weekly. On Sundays, I write a note to my sponsor explaining how many days and minutes I have written and exercised in the past week. I am not perfect about this. There have been many weeks where I failed to turn in a report and have had to do a two-week report. I never combine more than two weeks in one report. There is something essential about keeping records and sharing them with someone. It's what keeps me on track as a writer.

I write from the first day of my research projects. When I was teaching, I used to ask students on the day we started talking about term papers, "When would the best time be to start writing about your term paper topic?" Of course, the right answer was, "Right now!" and we would all pull out our pens and start brainstorming. Now that I work mostly with faculty as writers, my philosophy hasn't changed much. And that applies to me as a writer, too. When I first begin thinking about a topic, I get out my computer and start brainstorming. Then I choose between topics by comparing my brainstorming on one topic to the brainstorming on another. By having something on paper, I am also able to move forward with my research because, once something is written, it's much easier to criticize, revise, and ratchet it up to the next level. The "something" that I have on paper is likely to be PowerPoint™ slides. Other scholars may find this technique useful as well. You might create a simple set of PowerPoint™ slides and then write a paper from it. Of course, this is not too different from working from an outline, except it really encourages you to say your ideas out loud before writing them down, which can be enormously helpful.

I keep my thesis posted in the header or footer of each paper. Posting it there helps me remember to write a thesis sentence. It also helps me remember to work back and forth between my thesis and my paper, improving first one and then the other.

Just as organizing the paper around a key sentence (thesis) is helpful, organizing each paragraph around a key sentence is helpful, too. I don't know why my paragraphs were so incoherent before, but they were. The key sentences brought my paragraphs into focus. More important, it brought my thinking into focus. It also helped me limit my ideas to one point per paragraph. I had always tried to be organized by keeping outlines. In these outlines I synthesized the essence of each paragraph. But my reader wasn't privy to those outlines. Putting my key points in key sentences made my outlines accessible to my reader.

Next, I line up my key sentences to make an after-the-fact outline. I go through the after-the-fact outline carefully, checking first for purpose and audience. Does every sentence help me convey the purpose to the audience? Next, I check for organization, by which I mean logic and coherence. Have I said everything once and only once? Is it ordered in the most logical way? Is it coherent? Do the paragraphs stick together as well as is possible? I spend a lot of hours with this step and see a huge improvement in my writing.

I share my work with every manner of expert, including non-experts such as whole classrooms of undergraduates. Over a period of thirty months, I shared this book with a half-dozen of each of the following: writing groups (non-experts), experts, and Experts. For an ordinary academic article, I would share with only three or so people in each category. People remark most on my sharing of my manuscripts with Capital-E Experts. I go straight to the top. I invite the people whom I respect the most– on my side of the debate and on the other side–to read my work. I learn a lot from both groups. I try to share my manuscripts in the spirit of what Henry Eyring (1997) called a great learner:

> The first habit of great learners is to welcome correction. You've noticed that in the people around you who seem to be learning most.... [Great learners] see that everyone they meet knows something they don't. (pp. 3–6)

I also try to respond to every specific comment, but I regularly fail. I often set aside a comment because I don't understand how to respond to it or I am resisting it. I have a vague sense that the reader is probably right about something, but I don't know what to do about it or I think I have a better reason for leaving it the way it is. Later on someone will say something similar, and I realize that I should have made the change sooner. So I'm not as good at making a response to every specific comment as I could be. I should probably ask more questions of my readers until I understand more and can see yet a third way that accommodates my reason for how it is as well as the reader's reason for a change.

I do read my work out loud before sending it off–or listen to it read out loud to me. As long as I was reading out loud to myself, I found this tedious and I dreaded it. But it reduces my verbiage a lot and gives me a different window to my work so I forced myself to do it, whether I liked it or not. It was my least favorite step. Then I decided that I hated this step so much because I was reading out loud to myself. I have now convinced my partner, also a writer, to read our prose out loud to each other. Now I like reading out loud better. Or more accurately, I like having my work read out loud to me while I follow along. Involving someone else in this step makes this a much better experience because I learn from this important step, as I always did, but now I learn more and enjoy it more, too.

I do eventually kick every article or book out the door. Only three times in my life have I decided against sending something forward. Even in these instances, I decided against it rather than procrastinating. I decided that the works had fatal flaws and that my time would be better spent on other projects. In all three cases, I still think I was right. So I don't have any unfinished projects waiting to be finished. I do have a few ideas that I have not started seriously yet.

I know before I send a manuscript off that if it comes back rejected, I will send it off again, and where. So I have my next move in mind as a way of being prepared for rejection. And I certainly query the editor before I send a journal article off. It's invaluable. Sometimes I am rejected, but sometimes I am encouraged to submit the article and then I have much more confidence that it will be accepted. Querying editors has reduced the stress of publishing a lot for me.

When it comes time to send something off, I do hesitate because I feel scared. But I remind myself of a definition of courage I once heard. Courage means you're scared, but you do it anyway. So I'm scared, but I kick it out the door!

Appendix A
WRITING LOG

Week Beginning on _____   Name _____

	Mon	Tues	Wed	Thurs	Fri	Sat (opt.)	Sun (opt.)	Total
Writing Time (e.g. 8:15–8:45)								X
Minutes of Writing (e.g., 30)								

Note: "Writing time" includes any time working to communicate your research with words, such as outlining, revising, editing, writing paragraphs that will someday appear in the final paper, writing paragraphs that will never appear in the final paper, and writing the final presentation (not the generation) of numbers in tables or graphs.

WORKING THE STEPS

THIS WEEK I...

_____ wrote _____ days.

_____ recorded my minutes spent writing daily.

_____ shared my records with my sponsor or buddy. (This should be done daily for 90 days, until you establish a habit, and weekly thereafter.)

_____ posted my thesis on the wall (or, better, in my header or footer) and wrote to it; that is, my thesis was in plain view and I kept it in mind as I wrote.

_____ found a key sentence in every paragraph I wrote or revised.

_____ studied *only* my key sentences and asked: Does each key sentence support the purpose (thesis) of the paper? Are the key sentences organized (that is, are they logical and coherent)?

_____ shared a draft with someone.

_____ responded to each specific comment I was given.

_____ read my prose out loud.

_____ kicked a paper out the door by sending it to a co-author or to a journal or other publication outlet.

Appendix B
Finding Key Sentences in Paragraphs

Practice finding key sentences in the following paragraphs. As you read, feel free to refer back to the text about the characteristics of an ideal key sentence. Once you find the best available key sentence for each paragraph, write the number of the sentence in the left margin. For example, if the key sentence is first, write the numeral "1." If you don't think the paragraph has a key sentence at all, write "0" but then write a key sentence and show where it should be inserted. Be sure to complete each of the three paragraphs before reading further because the answers and their explanations appear immediately after the examples.

Example 1. By definition the true value for each of the unknown variance parameters must be positive. However, it is not uncommon to obtain some estimates of these parameters that are negative. In this study, negative estimates were handled using the Brennan approach (1983). Brennan's approach involves replacing the negative estimate with zero, but retaining the original negative estimate in the formula for estimating other variance components. This approach has the advantage of producing unbiased estimates of the other variance components.

Example 2. "The United States is at present the world's largest exporter of agricultural products. Its agricultural net balance of payments in recent years has exceeded $10 billion a year. As rising costs of imported petroleum and other goods have increased the U.S. trade deficit, this agricultural surplus has taken on great financial importance in both the domestic and international markets. First, agricultural exports maintain profitable market prices for the American farmer and bolster the national economy by providing over one million jobs. The

income from farm exports alone is used to purchase about
$9 billion worth of domestic farm machinery and equipment
annually. Exports of U.S. agricultural products also reduce price-
depressing surpluses. Without exports the government would
be subsidizing American farmers by more than $10 billion a
year over the current rate. Finally, agricultural exports provide
an entry to foreign markets than can be exploited by other
industries." (Williams, 1990, p. 100)

Example 3. "Seven out of eight reigns of the Romanov line after
Peter the Great were plagued by some sort of palace revolt
or popular revolution. In 1722, Peter the Great passed a law
of succession that terminated the principle of heredity. He
proclaimed that the sovereign could appoint a successor in order
to accompany his idea of achievement by merit. This resulted in
many tsars not appointing a successor before dying. Even Peter
the Great failed to choose someone before he died. Ivan VI was
appointed by Czarina Anna, but was only two months old at
his coronation in 1740. Elizabeth, daughter of Peter the Great,
defeated Anna, and she ascended to the throne in 1741. Succession
not dependent upon authority resulted in boyars' regularly
disputing who was to become sovereign. It was not until 1797 that
Paul I codified the law of succession: male primogeniture. But Paul
I was strangled by conspirators, one of whom was probably his
son, Alexander I." (Williams, 1990, p. 88)

As you read the answers below, don't feel bad if you "miss" an
answer because finding key sentences is not so much a test of your
reading skills as of the author's writing skills. In a well-written
paragraph, the key sentence is easy to find. If the key sentence is
not easy to find, then the paragraph needs revising.

Explanation 1. The first sentence explains that in theory the
estimates should always be positive; the second explains that
in fact they are not always positive. (A full paragraph could
have been written about each of these sentences—and another

paragraph could have been inserted here explaining that there are many approaches to handling this problem. Instead, the writer continues to write in shorthand.) The third sentence is key because it states that in this paper the Brennan approach will be used to handle negative estimates. The rest of the paragraph explains how the Brennan approach works and that it generates unbiased estimates.

Explanation 2. The first two sentences talk about the size of the agricultural surplus; the reader learns that it is the biggest in the world and totals $10 billion a year. (Once again, the author could have written a paragraph about how big the surplus is. Instead, the author changed the subject to how important it is.) The third sentence is key because it introduces the idea that the size of the surplus is important. (The writer should "trim the end" (Williams, 1990, p. 68) of this sentence to put more emphasis on the words "great financial importance." It is these words that point the reader to the key sentence.) The rest of the paragraph then explains various aspects of the importance of the surplus: providing jobs, reducing price-depressing surpluses, subsidizing American farmers, and providing an entry to foreign markets.

Explanation 3. This paragraph has no key sentence. Worse, the first sentence invites us to think about "palace revolt or popular revolution." The paragraph isn't about palace revolt or popular revolution, it's about succession to the throne. Therefore, the first sentence should be rewritten to serve as a true key: "After Peter the Great died, seven out of eight reigns of the Romanov line were plagued by turmoil over disputed succession to the throne" (Williams, 1990, p. 95). This paragraph was designed to show us what a good key sentence can do for a bad paragraph. With this key sentence the whole paragraph should come into focus for you.

Appendix C
Using Your Word Processor to Create an After-the-Fact Outline

You can use Microsoft® Word 2003 or 2007 to hide all your text except the key sentences and headings on either a PC or a Macintosh®. This will allow you to view or to print only your key sentences and headings without the rest of the text.

Instructions to Hide Text for Microsoft® Word 2003 on a PC:

1. Make sure your document will show hidden text.
   Select "Tools" on your toolbar and then select "Options." Next, select the "View" tab and then select the box next to "Hidden Text."

2. Hide all of the text in your document.
   Select all text in the document by selecting Ctrl+A (or by choosing "Select All" from the "Edit" menu). Then press Ctrl+D (alternately, select "Font" from the "Format" menu). When the font window opens, select "Hidden."

3. Unhide each heading and each key sentence.
   Select the text of the heading or key sentence you want to unhide and press Ctrl+D as before. When the font window opens, deselect "Hidden."

4. Choose to view ONLY the headings and key sentences (to see the outline of your paper).
   Select "Tools" on your toolbar and then select "Options." Next, select the "View" tab, and then deselect the box next to "Hidden Text."

Instructions to Hide Text for Microsoft® Word 2007 on a PC:

1. Make sure your document will show hidden text.
    Click on the Microsoft Office icon button in the upper left
    corner of the screen. Click on the "Word Options" button in the
    bottom right of the drop box. Then click on the "Display" tab
    on the left side. Check the box next to "Hidden Text" under the
    category "Always show these formatting marks on the screen."

2. Hide all the text in your document.
    Select all the text in the document by selecting Ctrl+A (or by
    selecting the "Home" tab and in the "Editing" section clicking
    on "Select" and choosing "Select All"). Then press Ctrl+D (or
    select the "Home" tab. In the bottom right corner of the "Font"
    section click on the arrow in a box.) In the box that will appear
    check the box next to the "Hidden" option.

3. Unhide each heading and each key sentence.
    Select the text of the heading or key sentence you want to
    unhide and press Ctrl+D as before. When the font window
    opens, deselect "Hidden."

4. Choose to view ONLY the headings and key sentences (to see
    the outline of your paper).
    Click on the Microsoft Office icon button in the upper left
    corner of the screen. Click on the "Word Options". Then click
    on the "Display" tab. Deselect the "Hidden Text" option.

Instructions to Hide Text for Microsoft® Word 2004 on a Macintosh®:

1. Make sure your document will show hidden text.
    Select "Preferences" from the Word menu. Make sure "View" is
    highlighted on the left-hand side, and then select "Hidden text"
    under the Nonprinting Characters.

2. Hide all of the text in your document.
    Select all text in the document by selecting Command+A (or
    by choosing "Select All" from the "Edit" menu). Then press

Command+D (alternately, select "Font" from the "Format" menu). When the font window opens, select "Hidden."

3. Unhide each heading and each key sentence.
Select the text of the heading or key sentence you want to unhide and press Command+D as before. When the font window opens, deselect "Hidden."

4. Choose to view ONLY the headings and key sentences (to see the outline of your paper).
Select "Preferences" from the Word menu. Make sure "View" is highlighted on the left-hand side, and then deselect Hidden text under the Nonprinting Characters.

Instructions to Hide Text for Microsoft® Word 2008 on a Macintosh®:

1. Make sure your document will show hidden text. Under the "Word" menu, click on "Preferences." Under "Authoring and Proofing Tools" click on "View." Under "Nonprinting characters" check the box next to "Hidden Text."

2. Hide all the text in your document.
Select all the text in the document by selecting Command+A (or "Select All" under the "Edit" menu). Then press Command+D (or select "Font" under the "Format" menu). In the box that appears, check the box next to the "Hidden" option.

3. Unhide each heading and each key sentence. Select the text of the heading or key sentence you want to unhide. Press Command+D (or select "Font" under the "Format" menu). In the box that appears, uncheck the box next to the "Hidden" option.

4. Choose to view ONLY the headings and key sentences to see the outline of your paper. Under the "Word" menu, click on "Preferences." Under "Authoring and Proofing Tools" click on "View." Under "Nonprinting characters" uncheck the box next to "Hidden Text." Click the "Show" button on the document tool bar to show/hide the hidden text.

Appendix D
Sample Letter to a Capital-E Expert

Dear Dr. Williams:

In 1992, I heard you speak at the University of Chicago at the 21st National Institute on Teaching and Learning. By then, I had read and studied [your book] *Style* a great deal. It taught me how to clean up my sentences!

I've been traveling with a workshop I present to faculty about their writing. I was teaching a *Writing Across the Curriculum* workshop, but in 1998, on a whim, I decided to teach something of what I knew about writing to help faculty themselves write better. I had observed that my peers didn't know as much as I wish they did about writing and weren't especially interested in my *Writing Across the Curriculum* workshop.

I established a program called *Publish and Flourish*, in which I teach certain steps about how to write well and revise rapidly and then ask participants to apply these steps to each other's work.

My two steps on revising owe much to your book *Style: Toward Clarity and Grace,* especially the two chapters with Greg Colomb on coherence. These are Steps 6 and 7: *Organize Around Key Sentences* and *Use Key Sentences as an After-the-Fact Outline.*

I have now written the workshop into a short book. I would appreciate it if you would read and comment on it, especially Steps 6 and 7, which owe the most to your work. (A story about you also appears in Step 8: *Share Early Drafts with Non-experts and Later Drafts with Experts.*)

You will notice that I use the idea of the POINT (key sentence) a little differently than you do. I tried using it exactly as you suggest but had some challenges that resulted in my modifying the idea a bit. Right now I am eager to know what comments you have about how I have used the idea.

Also, please let me know if there is anything you think I should read and cite that I haven't.

I am not asking for a careful read with copious comments. Just run your eyes over it and tell me the biggest problems you see. In exchange, I promise to read and comment on anything you send to me.

Please let me know when I might expect to hear from you. I appreciate it greatly.

Cordially yours,

Tara Gray

Tara Gray

Appendix E
Getting Help from Writing Groups

To start a writing group, get a group of writers together yourself or with the help of the teaching center on your campus. Some writers know just who they want in their group. Others want help finding like-minded people who are highly motivated to join a writing group. To find such people, you might turn to your teaching center because some centers organize writing groups as part of their faculty development efforts. Teaching centers generally help you find the people to be in writing groups by hosting workshops about writing groups. The writing workshops pull people together and teach a system for sharing feedback. Systems keep the conversation between writers from degenerating into useless comments that do not help writers such as, "It looks good." Whenever you work with a group of writers, you will want to use a system to give each other feedback.

In the two feedback systems described below, writers from a variety of disciplines meet weekly to give feedback on a few pages or on a full manuscript. We call these the "few-pages" and "full-manuscript" models. I regularly travel with an opening workshop on the "few-pages" model and occasionally give a longer version of the workshop that includes the full-manuscript model as well (*Publish & Flourish* workshops are described at www.taragray.com).

In the few-pages model, three or four writers meet for one hour per week to examine three pages of prose from every writer in the group. Each writer brings the pages he or she wrote that week. When your "few pages" are read, you lead the group.

When you ask the following questions, you are looking for the reader's most important ideas. Less important ideas, such as alternative word choices, should be noted on the manuscript and given to the writer after the session. In this way, you avoid tying up time by discussing less important ideas.

For the first five minutes, everyone (including you as the writer) reads the paper simultaneously while searching for key sentences. Searching for key sentences gives your colleagues a "reason to read" and gets them into the text even though the discipline may be far removed from their own. Searching for your own key sentences with an audience present also reveals some new insights, much like watching yourself speak on recorded video.

In the next nine minutes, ask your colleagues to discuss the paper with you by telling you which sentence is key in each paragraph—and why. If your prose is in good shape, your readers will be confident in their choices—and they will choose the same key sentences you chose. When they choose different key sentences, ask your readers why they chose the sentences they chose. Whether or not they choose different key sentences, close this section by asking, "What else in this paragraph?"

In the last minute, ask, "What works in this paper?" "What aspects should I keep as I make changes?" Remember to give this question the full one-minute period. Do not use it to make more criticisms. In all that you say, remember that the main purpose of writing groups is to motivate the writer to want to write more. This is especially true of this question.

The "few-pages" model has some advantages and one important drawback. The model spurs you to write daily because you are supposed to share new writing each week. Because only a few pages are reviewed by your peers at a time, when you return to your manuscript, you will find you can make the changes your readers prompted in about an hour. And you will find yourself writing paragraphs with this revision technique in mind so that what began as a revision technique becomes a better way of writing. Participants like this model because it requires no homework in terms of reading for other people. On the other hand, it is not as good at helping writers see the "big picture" issues as the full-manuscript model described below. (For a set of instructions about the "few pages" model that you could share with a writing group, see *Appendix F*.)

The "full-manuscript" model helps scholars focus on the big picture issues: purpose, audience, and large-scale organization. It was developed by Libby Rankin (2001) and modified by me using the work of Wayne Booth, Gregory Colomb and Joseph Williams (2003). In the full-manuscript model, three or four scholars meet for one hour weekly for 3-4 weeks. Each week, the group discusses one person's full manuscript. By discussing a whole paper, the focus is on the big picture issues. Each week one writer gives the group a paper to read for the next week along with a cover letter that describes the purpose and audience for the paper and poses questions for the group.

During the meeting readers ask questions and make comments in rounds. Once again, these rounds are led by the writer. One round involves something each person liked about the paper; another round involves answering the stated questions of the author; another round involves other questions, comments, or suggestions; the final round is another positive round, the "motivational round," that is designed to help the writer want to write some more. After a session using the full-manuscript model, when you return to your manuscript as a writer, you will find that you have learned much about what readers need in the way of seeing the big picture without losing the proverbial forest for the trees. (For a set of instructions about the "full-manuscript" model that you could share with a writing group, see *Appendix G.*)

Appendix F
Instructions for Writing Groups

"Few Pages Model"

Before you start:

- Discuss your weekly writing logs briefly.

- Divide time evenly between writers (as in 3:00–3:20, 3:20–3:40, etc.).

- Appoint a time keeper to help you stick to your schedule like glue.

- Review ground rules for readers and writers.

Ground Rules:

- *Readers:* Avoid passing judgment on what you read. Just tell which sentence seems to be key and why you think so or why you are unclear between two sentences. In all that you say, remember that the main purpose of writing groups is to motivate the writer to want to write more. Asking, "Do you mean X or Y here?" is more motivating to a writer than saying, "This is unclear" because the writer doesn't always know what is unclear or how to make it clear.

- *Writers:* During the time that your paper is discussed, focus your attention on listening, asking questions, taking notes, and moderating. Moderating should empower you and should help reduce the "sting" of having your work criticized. Instructions for how to moderate are below, but the most important thing is this: Avoid talking too much and explaining what you were trying to say. Instead, just look at the words on the paper and try to see your words through the reader's eyes. (If you do find yourself explaining what you were trying to say, be sure to write it down; it's usually clearer than what is on the paper.)

First five minutes: Read and search for keys

- *Readers:* Identify a key sentence (by number) for each paragraph.
- *Writers:* Pretend you are just another reader and do the exact same things the other readers are doing.

Second five minutes (or more): Discuss keys

- The writer asks, "In paragraph #1, which sentence is the key (#1, #2, #3, etc)?"
- If readers disagree, discussion ensues on that question before proceeding to the next question.
- If readers agree, the writer skips ahead to the next question, "What else in this paragraph?"
- Repeat for each paragraph.

Third five minutes (or less): The positive round

- The writer asks, "What works in this paper?" "What aspects should I keep as I make changes?"

Hints for Successful Writing Groups:

Before You Come:

- Write your thesis in the header or footer of your paper.
- Make four copies of a three-page rough draft.
- Find–but don't mark–your key sentence for every paragraph.

When You Arrive:

- Be on time.
- Pass your writing log around to your teammates and look at theirs. Discuss.
- If you forgot your writing log, create one on the spot.

Create a community of scholars

Appendix G
Instructions for Writing Groups

*Full-Manuscript Model**

*in the tradition of Elizabeth Rankin (2001), as well as Wayne Booth, Gregory Colomb, and Joseph Williams (2003)

Writer's Worksheet

As the writer, please attach a draft of an article-length manuscript to this completed writer's worksheet for your group to read before the next meeting.

Understand that your group is committed to spending no more than one hour with your manuscript so they will read carefully the most important parts of the paper–the title, abstract, headings, intro, and conclusion–but just skim or skip the rest of the paper.

Prepare yourself in advance of meeting with your group not to explain, argue, or defend your writing so you can spend your time listening and taking notes.

To Prepare:

First, go through all the questions the reader will be asking about your paper [see the next page] and ask them of yourself. Fix the problems you discover now so that you can give your readers a cleaner copy of your paper. This will mean you get more out of your time with the writing group.

Second, complete the following:

Audience for your paper:

The draft of the manuscript (first, middle, next-to-last, etc.):

The questions I have for you: (These questions should not require a detailed reading of the middle section of the paper because the group's attention will be focused on the introduction and conclusion. The questions should also avoid "yes/no" answers, as in, "Is the paper well organized?" in favor of wordings that invite more discussion, e.g., "As you look at the headings of the paper, do you think X should be placed with Y?")

Writer: Always attach the next page for the reader.

Reader's Worksheet

As a reader, you are well prepared for the group when you have at least something jotted down in each of the spaces below so that you could speak first on any round.

During the group meeting, you won't take time to discuss sentence-level changes, but your written comments are welcome and you are encouraged to give your copy of the paper to the writer at the end of the meeting.

Positive Round. Note something very specific that you really liked here. It can be something about content, organization, voice, or style. It's OK if someone else has already made your positive comment. Be sure to say it again because it's good reinforcement. Do not leave this blank! Write something!

Read Out Loud Round. During this round, listen as the writer reads the abstract (and the first page if time allows) out loud. (By reading out loud to others, the reader feels strengths and weaknesses physically—in one's mouth when pronouncing words and in one's ears when hearing them—and learns the effects of the words by watching the listeners (Elbow & Belanoff, 1995, p. 14). Afterwards, discuss.

Abstract and Introduction Round. Abstracts and introductions traditionally provide the context for the problem, followed by the problem and the proposed solution (or the promise for a solution). Share ideas here for doing this more clearly or persuasively in the abstract or the introduction.

Introduction and Conclusion Round. The introduction and conclusion work together like bookends to make it clear what the problem is and why it is worth solving and to answer the question "So what?" Share ideas here for doing this more clearly or persuasively.

Thesis Round. A thesis statement should be short and memorable and summarize the main argument of the paper. It need not prove the point—the rest of the paper will do that—but should name it. Underline the thesis statement of the paper. What suggestions do you have for shortening or sharpening the thesis statement?

Title Round. Is there any way to better address the theme in the title?

Organization Round. Based on the headings of the paper alone, what other ways to organize the paper might be suggested by logic or coherence?

Writer's Questions. Use the writer's worksheet to jot down your answer to each question the writer posed.

What Else? Other comments, questions, suggestions. As always, keep a positive tone and make sure you deliver critical comments in the spirit of helpful feedback.

Motivational Round. What is said last tends to stick in the writer's mind. Remember that the single biggest purpose we serve as a writing group is to motivate people to want to write more! Write one thing here that you can say honestly to this writer to help him or her want to get right back to work on this project!

Recommended Readings

Most Highly Recommended

Boice, R. (2000). *Advice for new faculty members: Nihil nimus.* Boston: Allyn & Bacon.

For thirty years, Bob Boice has been the premier psychologist and faculty developer on scholarly writing. His work offers the best proof that writers become more productive when they write daily in short blocks of time and hold themselves accountable to others for doing so. For the best introduction to his work on this subject, read the scholarship section. Every scholar should read this book.

Williams, J. (with Colomb, G.). (1990). *Style: Toward clarity and grace.* Chicago: University of Chicago Press.

The Williams book is the best book for revising any kind of non-fiction at the sentence level, with two excellent chapters on coherence at the paragraph level and beyond. Every scholar should read this book too. [Don't buy the student version with a similar name but a different date and publisher because it lacks the two most important chapters for academics, with Gregory Colomb, about coherence at the paragraph level and beyond.]

Gopen, G. D., & Swan, J. A. (1990). The science of scientific writing. *American Scientist, 78,* 550–558.

The Gopen and Swan article applies the principles of the Williams book to the sciences.

McCloskey, D. (2000). *Economical writing (*2nd ed.). Prospect Heights, IL: Waveland Press.

Howard Becker says that this book tells writers "to say what they have to say clearly and economically, and then shows them how. Students can learn how to write so the professor will know what they mean and, more important, professors can learn how to write so that the rest of the world will know what they mean." Warning: this book is very funny. You will laugh out loud.

Book Chapters and Articles

Gray, T., & Birch, A. J. (2001). Publish, don't perish: A program to help scholars flourish. *To Improve the Academy, 19,* 268–284.

The paper describes how two universities established a program that helped a hundred faculty members apply the principles described in this book to their scholarship.

Chilton, S. (1999). The good reviewer. *Academe, 85*(6), 54–55.

The short article offers excellent advice for being a good reviewer, including ways to avoid acting as though you have "privileged access to the Truth." For example, he recommends typing your name on the review before you begin writing it as a way of keeping yourself honest (even though you may remove it later).

Fiske, D. W., & Fogg, L. (1990). But the reviewers are making different criticisms of my paper! Diversity and uniqueness in reviewer comments. *American Psychologist, 45,* 591–598.

The myth persists that comments by anonymous reviewers are less than valuable. This analysis debunks the myth and helps scholars overcome its debilitating effects.

Valian, V. (1985). Solving a work problem. In M. F. Fox (Ed.), *Scholarly writing and publishing* (pp. 99–110). Boulder, CO: Westview Press.

The chapter urges you to consider working on one research project at a time until you gain some momentum.

Books

Moxley, J., & Taylor, T. (Eds.). (1997). *Writing and publishing for academic authors.* Lanham, MD: Rowman and Littlefield.

The collection includes many excellent chapters on writing in different areas (humanities, social sciences, etc.) and writing in different genres (journals, books, etc.)

Becker, H. S. (1986). *Writing for social scientists.* Chicago, IL: University of Chicago Press.

Howard Becker is an internationally known sociologist. One chapter alone, "Get it Out the Door," is worth the price of the book.

Committee on Women in Psychology and Women's Program Office Public Interest Directorate. (1988). *Understanding the manuscript review proce. Increasing the participation of women.* Washington, DC: American Psychological Association.

This is an extremely useful collection of articles for scholars and especially fc psychologists and other social scientists. I especially learned from the articles "An Editor Looks for the Perfect Manuscript" and "Manuscript Faults and Review Board Recommendations: Lethal and Nonlethal Errors."

Elbow, P. (1998). *Writing with power: Techniques for mastering the writing process.* London, UK: Oxford University Press.

The book shows writers how to "reduce the frustrations of writing by harnessing the two opposite mentalities that are required: a creative, accepting, open, imaginative, yea-saying mentality; and a tough, critical, logical, nay-saying mentality" (from the back cover). The book takes the writers skillfully through the steps of writing, revising, and getting feedback.

Booth, W. C., Colomb, G. G., & Williams, J. M. (1995, 2003). *The craft of research.* Chicago, IL: The University of Chicago Press.

A book aimed at writing research papers, theses, and dissertations, but many faculty rave about it, too. The book helps scholars at all stages construct better research.

Baker, S. (1984). *The complete stylist and handbook.* New York, NY: Harper and Row.

An excellent textbook on writing that covers the big-picture issues of writing that are hardest, e.g. thinking about the paper as a whole and in sections, rather than as paragraphs and sentences. The book is aimed at beginning college students but useful to writers at all levels.

Keyes, R. (1995). *The courage to write.* New York, NY: Henry Holt & Co.

This book helps writers keep hope alive and keep writing. Chapter 5, "Finessing Fear," is about why writers write in such an obscure fashion, particularly in academe. The chapter, like the book, is funny, sobering, and enlightening all at once.

Shaughnessy, S. (1993). *Walking on alligators: A book of meditations for writers.* San Francisco, CA: HarperSanFrancisco.

Of all the books designed to motivate writers, Ralph Keyes calls this the best of the lot. He warns that every writer he knows would rather read the book than write.

Bird by bird: Some instructions on writing and life. New York,
Books.

bout the author's incredible journey as a writer. It is an
: treatment of dealing with perfectionism, finding your voice,
₵ a big project small. The book is entertaining and the advice is
nsical and refreshingly blunt.

⅃bs

tion Doctor by Dr. Sally Jensen.

ly Jensen provides dissertation coaching to those needing support and
,on beyond that which is provided by (some) dissertation advisors. See
.dissertationdoctor.com for more details.

Planning and Workaholism

, M. (1997). *Tomorrow's professor: Preparing for academic careers in*
ience and engineering. New York, NY: IEEE Press.

[his book provides advice on preparing for a career in academe in science
and engineering. The book shows how to find the right job, do the job right,
and get tenure.

This author maintains the best imaginable listserv that he bills as "desktop
faculty development 100 times a year." The listserv summarizes two books
per week. The topics covered include research, teaching and learning, career
planning, and other topics of interest to academics. The list can be subscribed
to at http://ctl.stanford.edu/Tomprof/index.shtml

assel, D. (1990). *Working ourselves to death and the rewards of recovery.* New
York, NY: Harper Paperbacks.

This book helps a scholar decide whether you talk about being overworked
mainly because it is a status symbol or because you seriously wonder whether
you might be working yourself to death. If you have any doubt, read this book.
Fassel identifies the many (sneaky) ways of working yourself to death and
points out that they don't all include incredible hours at your paid job.

Lazear, J. (2001). *The man who mistook his job for a life: A chronic overachiever finds the way home.* New York, NY: Crown Publishers.

This is a very hopeful book about one writer's work addiction and his successful efforts to overcome the problem and rejoin his life and his family. The book offers suggestions on how to approach the problem of work addiction and overcome it. For the work-addicted scholar, this book is a life saver.

Funding Your Best Ideas: A 12-Step Program

Joan Straumanis,
Former FIPSE Program Officer
Reprinted by Permission

Part I: Before Writing

1. Innovate—and if you can't think of anything brand new, do something unexpected. This is your angle; now feature it.

2. Do your homework. Find your niche. What are others doing about this issue? Show that you know, and place your project within this context.

3. Build a team. Mix things up. Build and cross bridges—among departments, disciplines and schools. Between academia and business. Between schools and colleges. Include students and administrators. Be generous: share work and ownership. Appoint an advisory committee of famous people in your field— to get a head start on dissemination—but don't give them much work to do, and you won't need to pay them very much.

4. Find the right funding agency. Know agency interests, culture, and style. Submit applications to more than one agency (but, of course, don't accept multiple grants supporting the same activities).

5. Use the phone. Call a program officer, briefly summarize your idea, and and prepare specific questions. Take the program officers's advice very seriously, but exercise your own best judgment. Some agencies are more directive than others.

Part II: While Writing

6. Use a journalistic writing style. Use the "W" words of journalism: Who, what, when, where, why and how. Also use bullets, lists, outlines, diagrams, tables. Don't obsess on any topic, even if important. Make it interesting; let every sentence

do a job. Assume that your reviewer is reading in bed, falling asleep–which is very likely true.

7. Follow guidelines to the letter. Keep them before you as you write (but don't quote them back to the agency). Match headings in the proposal to headings in the guidelines so the reader doesn't have to hunt for needed information. Use "signposts": I am about to explain why... I have just argued that...

8. Build in continuation, evaluation, and dissemination. Factory installed, not an add-on and not postponed to the last year. Continuation plans are an indicator of institutional commitment. Evaluation should be independent and objective, but doesn't need to meet standards of the *Journal of Psychometrics*–use common sense. What would you want to know about the success of an idea before you would consider adopting it? Evaluate "politically"–i.e., with an eye toward later publicity. What would you want to see in headlines? Note the difference between passive and active dissemination. (The first disseminates admiration, not innovation.)

9. Watch the bottom line. Share costs. Know how to cut costs without hurting the project: request replacement salaries instead of released time, charge actual instead of estimated benefits, follow agency recommendations on indirect costs.

10. Leverage funds. Solicit funds from third parties, contingent on grant funding. This can be done in advance (to beef up cost share and make proposal more attractive), as well as after project is funded.

11. Get a sharp (toothed) reader. Best: someone unfamiliar with your field, your project. Not an editor/proofreader. Have them read final draft without taking notes. Then ask them to tell you– from memory–what the project will do, how it will do it, why it is significant, and how it is different. Rewrite proposal if these answers aren't clear and correct, or they don't flow effortlessly.

12. Write the abstract last. Put in your key innovation. Write three versions: one page (first page of proposal, whether requested or not), one paragraph (if requested), and one line, the proposal title–which you should think of as a mini-abstract (descriptive and intriguing). Don't repeat abstract or proposal text. Prepare for the possibility that some sleepy reviewer might read only the abstract.

Other good advice:

- Request reviews. Use the phone to ask agency staff why the project was or was not funded. If you are rejected, you can always try again.

- If you get funded, let your agency help you. Brainstorming. Troubleshooting. Running interference with administration. Leveraging funds. Making you famous.

- Help your agency.

References

Association of Learned and Professional Society Publishers. (2000). *Current practice in peer peview: Results of a survey conducted during Oct/Nov 2000.* Retrieved from http://www.alpsp.org

Baker, S. (1984). *The complete stylist and handbook.* New York, NY: Harper and Row.

Beattie, M. (1987). *Codependent no more: How to stop controlling others and start caring for yourself.* New York, NY: Harper.

Becker, H. S. (1986). *Writing for social scientists.* Chicago, IL: University of Chicago Press.

Belcher, W. L. (2009). *Writing your journal article in 12 weeks: A guide to academic publishing success.* Los Angeles, CA: Sage.

Bernard, A. (Ed). (1990). *Rotten rejections.* Ossining, NY: Pushcart Press.

Boice, R. (1989). Procrastination, busyness and bingeing. *Behavior Research Therapy, 27*, 605–611.

Boice, R. (1990). *Professors as writers: A self-help guide to productive writing.* Stillwater, OK: New Forums Press.

Boice, R. (1994). *How writers journey to comfort and fluency.* Westport, CT: Praeger.

Boice, R. (1997). Strategies for enhancing scholarly productivity. In J. M. Moxley & T. Taylor, (Eds.), *Writing and publishing for academic authors* (pp. 19–34). Lanham, MD: Rowman and Littlefield.

Boice, R. (2000). *Advice for new faculty members: Nihil nimus.* Boston, MA: Allyn & Bacon.

Booth, W. C., Colomb, G. G., & Williams, J. M. (1995, 2003). *The craft of research.* Chicago: The University of Chicago Press.

Carroll, G. (1969). *Principles of good writing.* Westport, CT: Famous Writers School.

Covey, S. R. (1989). *The 7 habits of highly effective people: Powerful lessons in personal change.* New York, NY: Simon and Schuster.

Drake, S. M., & Jones, G. A. (1997). *Writing your way to success : Finding your own voice in academic publishing.* Stillwater, OK: New Forums Press.

Dutton, D. (n.d.). *The bad writing contest: Press releases, 1996–1998.* Retrieved from http://www.denisdutton.com/bad_writing.htm

Dutton, D. (1999, February 5). Language crimes: A lesson in how not to write. [Electronic version]. *The Wall Street Journal.* Retrieved from http://www.denisdutton.com/language_crimes.htm

Elbow, P. (1973). *Writing without teachers.* London, UK: Oxford University Press.

Elbow, P. (1998). *Writing with power.* London, UK: Oxford University Press.

Elbow, P. (2000). The believing game: A challenge after 25 years. In P. Elbow, (Ed.), *Everyone can write essays: Toward a hopeful theory of writing and teaching writing* (pp. 76–80). London, UK: Oxford University Press.

Elbow, P., & Belanoff, P. (1995). *Sharing and responding.* New York, NY: McGraw-Hill.

Eyring, H. B. (1997, October). *Brigham Young University Speeches 1997–98: A child of God.* Provo, UT: Brigham Young University. Retrieved from http://speeches.byu.edu/?act=viewitem&id=747

Fassel, D. (1990). *Working ourselves to death and the rewards of recovery.* New York, NY: Harper Paperbacks.

Fiske, D. W., & Fogg, L. (1990). But the reviewers are making different criticisms of my paper! Diversity and uniqueness in reviewer comments. *American Psychologist, 45,* 591–598.

Flower, L., Stein, V., Ackerman, J., Kantz, M. J., McCormick, K., & Peck, W. C. (Eds). (1990). *Reading-to-write: Exploring a Cognitive and Social Process.* New York, NY: Oxford University Press.

Forster, E. M. (1973). *Aspects of the novel.* New York, NY: Harcourt, Brace & World (Original work published 1927)

Foss, S. K., & Waters, W. (2007). *Destination Dissertation: A Traveler's Guide to a Done Dissertation.* Lanham, MD: Rowman & Littlefield Publishers.

Goldman, B. (2001, September 5). *Summer workshop provides success strategies for future professors* [Electronic version]. Retrieved from http://www.stanford.edu/group/AIM/workshops/archives/FPMstrategies.html

Gopen, G. D., & Swan, J. A. (1990). The science of scientific writing. *American Scientist, 78,* 550–558.

Gray, T. (1998). Your students can too write—and you can show them how. *Journal of Criminal Justice Education, 9,* 131–139.

Gray, T. (1999). Publish, don't perish: Twelve steps to help scholars flourish. *Journal of Staff, Program and Organization Development, 16,* 135–142.

Gray, T., & Birch, A. J. (2001). Publish, don't perish: A program to help scholars flourish. *To Improve the Academy, 19,* 268–284.

Harker, W. J. (1982). Publishing in Canada. In S. Judy, (Ed.), *Publishing in English education* (pp. 112–126). Portsmouth, NH: Boynton.

Henson, K. T. (1997, June). Writing for publication: Some perennial mistakes. *Phi Delta Kappan,* 781–784.

Henson, K. T. (1999). *Writing for professional publication: Keys to academic and business success.* Boston, MA: Allyn & Bacon.

Hollingsworth, S. (2002). Writing and publishing. In J. E. Cooper & D. D. Stevens, (Eds.), *Tenure in the sacred grove: Issues and strategies for women and minority faculty* (pp. 147–161). Albany, NY: State University of New York Press.

Keyes, R. (1995). *The courage to write.* New York, NY: Henry Holt & Co.

Lazear, J. (2001). *The man who mistook his job for a life: A chronic overachiever finds the way home.* New York, NY: Crown.

McCloskey, D. (1985). Economical writing. *Economic Inquiry, 23,* 187–222.

McCloskey, D. (2000). *Economical writing,* (2nd ed.). Prospect Heights, IL: Waveland Press.

Menges, R. J. (1999). Dilemmas of newly hired faculty. In R. J. Menges and Associates (Eds.), *Faculty in new jobs* (pp. 19-38). San Francisco, CA: Jossey-Bass.

Mills, C. W. (1959). On intellectual craftsmanship. In C. W. Mills, (Ed.), *The sociological imagination* (pp. 195–226). New York, NY: Grove.

Moxley, J. M. (1997). If not now, when? In J. M. Moxley & T. Taylor, (Eds.) *Writing and publishing for academic authors* (pp. 3–13). Lanham, MD: Rowman and Littlefield.

Moxley J. M., & Taylor, T. (Eds.) (1997). *Writing and publishing for academic authors.* Lanham, MD: Rowman and Littlefield.

Olson, G. A. (1997). Publishing scholarship in humanistic disciplines. In J. M. Moxley & T. Taylor (Eds.), *Writing and publishing for academic authors* (pp. 51–69). Lanham, MD: Rowman and Littlefield.

Quintilian. (1980). *Institutio oratoria.* Book VIII. Cambridge, MA: Harvard University Press.

Rankin, E. (2001). *The work of writing: Insights and strategies for academics and professionals.* San Francisco, CA: Jossey-Bass.

Shaughnessy, S. (1993). *Walking on alligators: A book of meditation for writers.* San Francisco, CA: HarperSanFrancisco.

Smaby, M. H., Downing, T., & Crews, J. (1999). Publishing in scholarly journals: Part II–Is it an attitude or technique? It's a technique. *Counseling Education and Supervision Journal, 38,* 227–235.

Thyer, B. A. (1994). *Successful publishing in scholarly journals.* Thousand Oaks, CA: Sage.

Van Til, W. (1986). *Writing for professional publication* (2nd ed.). Boston, MA: Allyn and Bacon, Inc.

Von Bekesy, G. (1960). *Experiments in hearing.* New York, NY: McGraw–Hill.

Webb, D. (1996–1999). "The way things work." Stray Lines in a Curvature. *The Wine Press Poetry Pages.* Retrieved from http://winepress.com/StrayLines_12.htm

Weiss, A. (2002, November). *The odd couple: Marketing and strategy skills for speakers.* Workshop presented in San Francisco.

Williams, J. (with Colomb, G.). (1990). *Style: Toward clarity and grace.* Chicago, IL: The University of Chicago Press.

Index

129

Do You Want Feedback on a Manuscript?

Manuscript and Writing Guidance
by Rene Hadjigeorgalis

We've all lived the drill. We work for months on end on a manuscript, finally let it go, and send it to the reviewer. We receive the reviewer's comments only to find out that he missed the entire point of our manuscript.

It's easy to blame reviewers. They are normally faceless, and by most accounts not too pleasant in their comments. If it's not the reviewer, then it's the clueless thesis advisor. But is it really their fault? Is it at all possible that there was a "failure to communicate?"

"Of course not! I spent months on this! I had all of the experts in my field read it!"

Maybe you need a Non-Expert.

A non-expert is not constrained by your discipline. Non-experts are not drawn to the theory at the expense of your writing. Their role is to focus on your writing and whether or not you are saying what you set out to say. As a non-expert, I can help you to communicate your ideas by helping you:

- Avoid digressions
- Improve organization and clarity
- Uncover overriding (but often hidden) themes

I will read your manuscript with particular attention to these issues and provide you with written comments within a specified time. For an additional fee, I can discuss your paper with you further by telephone. Early, partial drafts as well as more refined manuscripts are welcome.

Rene Hadjigeorgalis is a former faculty member at a land-grant institution. She has reviewed manuscripts in aeronautical engineering, agronomy, biology, chemistry, civil engineering, computer science, economics, electrical engineering, English, faculty development, history, library science, linguistics, literature, management, mechanical engineering, nursing, public health, social work, sociology, soil science, Spanish, statistics, and teaching.

2008 Fee Schedule	Cost per Page*
Written Comments: 10 business-day turnaround	$6
Written Comments: 5 business-day turnaround	$8
Written Comments: 2 business-day turnaround	$10

Page count based on double-spaced text. Minimum charge of $50. Add $30 per manuscript for discussion by telephone.

Send manuscripts as attachments (Microsoft® Word or pdf) to:
Rene.Hadjigeorgalis@gmail.com

Teaching Academy Bookstore Order Form

(please print or type)

name

title

affiliation

physical mailing address (no box numbers)

city   state   zip

daytime telephone   alternate telephone

fax

e-mail

Item	Price	Qty	Extension
Publish & Flourish book	$25.00		
Publish & Flourish ❑ DVD ❑ Videotape	$50.00		
Publish & Flourish PowerPoint™ slides	$50.00		
Teaching at a Distance with the Merging Technologies	$54.00		
KnowledgeDollar$: The Business of Consulting	$29.95		
Engaging Students in Distance Learning: Interactive activities and exercises for field sites	$24.95		
Shipping (see below)			
Total-			

Shipping: $8 shipping & handling for the first item and $2 for each additional item will be added to each order to ship UPS Ground within the continental U.S. Call 575/646–2204 to request information about other shipping options.

Payment

❑ Check   ❑ Purchase order # _____

Charge my credit card:

❑ VISA   ❑ MasterCard   ❑ Discover

credit card number   expiration date

signature

Purchase order and credit card purchases may be faxed to 575/646–1330. Orders paid by check may be mailed to:

**Teaching Academy MSC 3TA
New Mexico State University
P.O. Box 30001
Las Cruces NM 88003-8001**

www.teaching.nmsu.edu